CLASSIC DECORATIVE
DETAILS

CLASSIC DECORATIVE DETAILS

HENRIETTA SPENCER-CHURCHILL

Little, Brown and Company (Canada) Limited

Boston / New York / London / Toronto

DEDICATION

To my two sons, David and Maximilian, who provide such enthusiasm about my work and the writing of a new book, and who give me endless encouragement.

To my mother, Susan Gough, from whom I have learnt so much about detail and who is a constant source of inspiration.

To my father, 'Sunny' John George Vanderbilt Henry Spencer-Churchill, 11th Duke of Marlborough, from whom I have learnt to appreciate the beauty of our past and use it in my work.

First published in Canada in 1994
by Little, Brown and Company (Canada) Limited

This paperback edition published 1996
by Little, Brown and Company (Canada) Limited
148 Yorkville Avenue
Toronto, Ontario
M5R 1C2

First published in Great Britain in 1994
by Anaya Publishers Ltd London

Editor Alexandra Parsons
Design Nigel Partridge
Picture researcher Philippa Lewis
Special photography Andreas von Einsiedel

1 3 5 7 9 8 6 4 2

Canadian Cataloguing in Publication Data
Spencer-Churchill, Henrietta, 1958-
        Classic decorative details
ISBN 0 316-14256-5
1. Interior decoration. I. Title.
NK2115.S64 1996   747   C96-931495-7

Typeset in Great Britain by Bookworm Typesetting, Manchester
Colour reproduction by HBM Print Pte Ltd, Singapore
Printed and bound in Singapore by CS Graphics Pte Ltd

AUTHOR'S ACKNOWLEDGEMENTS

My thanks go firstly to everyone at Anaya who has helped in creating
Classic Decorative Details, my second book with them. In particular I
would like to thank Carey Smith who has worked so hard in getting it
all together.
Secondly, I would like to thank my Editor, Alexandra Parsons, who
does a wonderful job in sorting my rather disjointed text into a much
more logical and readable format!
Thanks also go to Bill Batten for what is in my view, a beautiful jacket,
and to Andreas von Einsiedel for the specialist photography, Pippa
Lewis for her excellent work in picture research and Nigel Partridge for
the superb design and layout of the book.
I would also like to express my gratitude to Rizzoli, who successfully
published my first book *Classic English Interiors* in the U.S. and I look
forward to a repeat performance!

CONTENTS

ACKNOWLEDGEMENTS 191

INTRODUCTION

We are all individuals, our lifestyles are diverse, our senses of taste and colour differ and the homes we live in are all different. Your home should reflect your own styles and personality. Your individual stamp should shine through in the detail, the pictures, the objets d'art you have chosen to surround yourself with.

As an interior designer it is my job to understand my clients' needs and to influence them towards practical decisions. But at the same time I try and make certain that their own style is reflected in the overall design concept, and I encourage them to select the details, bearing in mind the architectural style of the house.

Starting a collection or even buying a painting can be a daunting process, especially if you are just starting out and feel unsure about taking the plunge and making commitments. But it is better you do it than have someone do it for you. You will soon gain confidence. Once you have seen your purchase in situ, and have received compliments about how good it looks, and how clever you were to find it at such a good price, you will be eager to prove youself again.

Collections cannot be formed overnight and few of us are lucky enough to inherit an instant home, and anyway half the fun in building a collection is the 'hunt' and the challenge involved, whether buying at markets, at auctions or in antique shops.

The key is to have the courage of your own convictions, and when you see something you like, buy it. The chances are that it will have gone by the time you go back a second time. If you suddenly discover that you have made a terrible mistake, it doesn't matter: you can always sell it again or give it away!

Remember it is the individual items that will transform your house into a home and reflect your personality and exude your style. So take time to concentrate on these important elements of homemaking and enjoy the process not only in your home town but on your travels all over the world. Objects collected on travels abroad will not only add another sense of style, but bring back fond memories of a trip or maybe a particular person.

I hope that in this book you will find ideas on forming collections and displaying them imaginatively and to their best advantage and discovering ways of achieving effects without feeling that you have to buy the best.

A collection of baskets can be just as decorative as a valuable set of Sèvres procelain – it is just making a different statement and reflecting another style. Equally an antique dresser with a display of contemporary blue and white china can be just as effective as one filled with antique pieces, so don't be put off by feeling that you have to buy old: after all our pieces of today will one day be antiques to our offspring!

Henrietta Spencer-Churchill

PICTURES AND MIRRORS

A ROOM WITHOUT IMAGES IS A ROOM WITHOUT LIFE AND WITHOUT CHARACTER. YOU CAN USE PICTURES TO MAKE STRONG STATEMENTS ABOUT YOUR PERSONAL STYLE, TO LIVEN UP DULL EXPANSES OF WALL, AND TO GIVE YOUR LIVING SPACES A DISTINCT CHARACTER AND CHARM. THE PICTURES THEMSELVES DO NOT HAVE TO BE EXPENSIVE: A LOT OF THEIR IMPACT COMES FROM IMAGINATIVE MOUNTING, HANGING AND LIGHTING.

✻✻✻✻✻✻✻✻✻✻✻✻✻✻✻✻✻✻✻✻✻✻✻✻✻✻✻✻✻✻✻✻✻✻✻✻✻

LIVING WITH IMAGES

Pictures and paintings complete a room, give it character, life and warmth. The choice of medium ranges from posters and prints to watercolours, oils and mixed media collages, and within these categories the choice of subject matter is such that you are bound to find something that epitomizes your style and taste.

Of course, we would all love to possess the real thing – an Old Master glowing with rich colour or a genuine Impressionist that captures the very atmosphere of spring – but such luxury is afforded to few. There are, however, many inexpensive alternatives. Antique markets yield pretty watercolours and witty prints that can be transformed with stylish mounts and frames. Auction houses are a good hunting ground for oil paintings and Art School shows are often the place to buy the work of promising new painters at affordable prices.

Motley collections of inherited pictures can either be sold and the money invested in an image you really want or, if the original pictures are pleasing to your eye, they may benefit from being remounted and re-framed to suit your style of decoration.

Whatever your taste in images, from challenging abstracts to play-it-safe prints – and you may decide to try

ABOVE A 17th century portrait is the focal point of a formal, gilded arrangement in a hall. The gilt wood marble-topped console table underneath it is flanked by two chairs in the French style. This shade of yellow sets off the gilt magnificently.

LEFT Making the most of prints means mounting them sensitively. The horse print has a green mount which picks up colour from the walls and from the print itself. The thin gold slip around the frame gives it a bit of sparkle and helps define it against the strong wallpaper. Small prints, like the two portraits on either side, look best with generous mounts.

BELOW The dragged lime green walls make a perfect background for this charming oil still life. The little silver tankards full of fresh wild flowers make the setting for this painting even more appealing.

BELOW Pristine white mounts and mahogany frames against a dark wall define these finely printed pages taken from an architectural pattern book.

ABOVE Here is an example of a boldly-striped wallpaper providing a dramatic background for a harmonious grouping, with the darkest painting in the centre to draw in the eye.

different approaches in different parts of the house – you need to be sure that the paintings or pictures you hang in your homes are images that give you constant pleasure.

BACKGROUNDS FOR PAINTINGS

To give your pictures a chance to shine, think carefully about the decoration of the walls on which you intend to hang them. A heavily-patterned wallpaper may clash with your images and an ill-chosen shade of paint may diminish their impact. This does not mean to say that all your walls should be painted art gallery white. Strong, plain colours usually work very well, bold stripes make a good background for large, important-looking paintings and small geometric or floral patterned wallpapers look particularly good as a background for mounted prints and watercolours.

ABOVE *Leaves from an oriental screen are flanked by Indian
'company' paintings produced by Indian artists for colonial clients:
officials of the British East India Company.*

FOCAL POINTS AND COLLECTIONS

A focal point is one towards which everyone's eyes are inexorably drawn as they enter a room. Choosing a single image for such prominent treatment is a matter of personal taste but it should be a strong image that is capable of standing alone and demanding attention. You can help give it the significance it needs with an interesting frame and by positioning it either over a fireplace or over a dominant piece of furniture. You should be able to see the picture from any part of the room and it should be well lit both by day and by night.

COLLECTIONS WITH A THEME

You may, on the other hand, elect to make your statement not with a single image but with a collection. A cohesive collection is one with some common strain running through it, either of medium or of message: a collection of watercolours, for instance, or of landscapes, illustrated bookplates or naive portraits of farm animals. Whatever the theme, a good collection will add up to more than the sum of its separate parts, as its impact depends largely on repetition. The pictures should not necessarily be of equal size and importance, nor is it obligatory to have them framed identically as the texture of a collection is enhanced by subtle differences.

ABOVE A charming collection of American folk art – a combination of Pennsylvania German paintings and scripts with their characteristic yellow, red and green colouring and simple tulip and bird motifs. The pictures look quite at home in sturdy frames on a plain whitewashed wall.

LEFT A themed collection of prints depict, in different ways, the same species of flower – auriculas – to give this guest bedroom a welcoming atmosphere. The collection is mixed with three-dimensional objects: a whimsical wooden bird in a garland of carved leaves and, to the right, parts of two monstrances.

MONTAGES ETCETERA

There are other things besides pictures that look good on a wall. An artfully arranged collection of masks, decorative hair combs, straw hats, dried flowers or shells can add three-dimensional interest to a room as well as providing a splash of colour and texture.

A montage is best described as a composite whole comprised of juxtaposed elements, and it is in the careful juxtaposition of these elements that the success or failure of a montage rests.

For a group of objects to have an impact they need to be harmoniously balanced and grouped, like a collection of pictures, into an overall shape. The relationship

BELOW *An impressive array of seals. Some are actual sealing wax impressions, some plaster casts of the impressions and some are the seals themselves. What could be a rather sterile collection is bought to vivid life by beautiful frames and mounts made from pages of old documents.*

RIGHT *Three little pink-tinged paintings form the backbone of this decorative arrangement of pink and glass.*

BELOW *A montage of Victorian busts symmetrically arranged on and around a mantelpiece. Recognizable among the Victorian English worthies are Sir Walter Scott, the Duke of Wellington and Prince Albert.*

between the objects will most often be one of function: old kitchen utensils or book jackets, for instance, and, as with any grouping of like objects, the spaces between them should be regular, as the grouping and spacing are very much part of the whole.

If your montage is based on objects related only through colour, texture or imagery – images of chickens, for instance, ranging from postcards to terrine dishes to enamel signs – then the large and the small must be carefully balanced, colour relationships need to be taken into consideration, and the whole should be held together with wit and a sense of fun.

Small objects may look best mounted in a fabric-covered box-type frame, or placed in a shallow wall cabinet which can then be hung on the wall and lit with a spotlight as if it were a serious painting.

CHILDREN'S ART

There is an age, somewhere between nursery school, when they first learn how to hold a paint brush, and the first year of secondary school, when spontaneity is often 'taught' out of them, when children paint what they imagine unselfconsciously. If you put a palette of colours in front of them, and give them a sheaf of paper sheets cut to fit a frame that is too big or too small for any other purpose – wide pine ones look particularly good – you may well end up with one or two charming, original naïfs for the price of a happy hour of daubing.

LIGHTING

Good lighting enhances a picture, casts it in a warm glow and shows it off to best advantage. Relying on general overhead lighting to do the job is not advisable. Good picture lighting does not cast shadows, does not cause annoying reflections on pictures protected by glass and does not shine into anyone's eyes.

DIRECT LIGHTING

There are basically two options when it comes to lighting pictures: direct or indirect light. Directional lighting, which means a specific light directed at a specific picture, needs to be planned well in advance as walls may have to be chased out and ceilings cut for wires and fittings to be installed. Perhaps the most efficient form of directional light comes from individual picture lights, which work well on oils. I prefer the brass ones that can be attached to the picture frame, throwing light downward, and I prefer the less obtrusive matt brass finish, which is more in keeping with antique gilded or carved frames, as opposed to shiny lacquered brass.

BELOW *A victorious St. George is bathed in heavenly luminosity thanks to an overhead picture light which brings out the bronze tones of the painting.*

You must choose the right size of light relative to the size of your painting, as one of the wrong size will shine on the painting at the wrong angle and cast shadows. Picture lights can also be fixed below the painting to cast light upwards, and this can look very effective with contemporary works of art.

Fixed wall-mounted picture lights are also available, but they give you less flexibility and, if too ornate, can distract from the picture.

There are now some excellent directional ceiling lights available, either as track-fixed spots or recessed downlighters. These can be pin-pointed onto the walls, and the area of light cast adjusted in shape and size to frame the picture or group of pictures.

ABOVE *A pair of candle sconces provide an appropriate source of indirect light for a 19th century romantic painting. These are, in fact, electrified, but they still cast a suitably dim romantic glow.*

INDIRECT LIGHTING

The light that spills from table lamps, standard lamps, reading lamps and uplighters can also be used to illuminate pictures. As indirect light from sources such as these tends to be reflected off other surfaces, it gives a less controllable but gentler light that may well cast shadows, but hopefully not harsh ones. Indirect light is the right choice for pictures under glass, as directional light will glare and flare on a reflective surface.

HANGING

The way in which pictures are hung is as much a matter of individual taste as the subject matter of the images. Some people will prefer a clutter of imagery while others favour a single image, standing alone. Important pictures certainly do look better on their own with space around them, good lighting and a prominent position in the room.

THE SITE AND THE HEIGHT

Consider the practical as well as the aesthetic when deciding where to hang your pictures. Avoid placing oils over radiators or in a room in which the temperature

ABOVE *A regal set of hand-coloured prints of British royalty hung very precisely as a group so they look like one image with repeating patterns.*

is likely to vary a great deal, as dryness and fluctuating temperatures are likely to cause the canvas to dry and the paint to crack. Watercolours and prints will fade if placed in direct sunlight, even if protected by glass. Damp conditions, such as those found in bathrooms and kitchens, will cause condensation to get behind the frame and cause foxing (spotting or discoloration of the paper).

I find it very irritating to see pictures hung off-centre above pieces of furniture. While not advocating symmetry, I do believe that pictures, and groups of pictures, should be centred on a wall or between two doorways as this helps to frame the frame. Another irritation is pictures that are hung too high. Where possible, pictures should be hung at the eye level of someone standing up. On staircases, the height should follow the rise of the stairs so that the eye level remains constant.

ARRANGING GROUPS

Having said all that about eye level, it is obviously not possible to get all the pictures in a group at one eye level, and there is no need to. There is nothing wrong in hanging pictures one above the other or in mixing oils, watercolours and prints of differing sizes, periods and framing styles. Again it is a matter of personal taste, but beware jarring mismatches such as a modern subject with a

ABOVE *Crowding their way up a curved staircase wall are a collection of drawings of different sizes, all in wooden frames with white or neutral-coloured mounts.*

LEFT *A regiment of 17th century British heroes arranged with military precision in identical black wooden frames.*

LEFT *This group of consists of pair of late 18th century stipple engravings, a pair of coloured mezzotints of birds and a pair of modern portraits. They hang in my sitting room where I have arranged them in an elongated, symmetrical oval, flanking a lovely dry point etching by Paul Hellu.*

BELOW *A set of 19th century colour plates from a pattern and ornament manual are hung in a neat row in this country-style kitchen.*

bright aluminium frame trying to look an integral part of a group of gilded frames and antique tapestries.

There are no hard-and-fast rules either as to whether larger paintings should be above or below the rest. What dictates the layout of a group is the size and shape of the pictures, the size of the wall and the way in which the furniture is grouped in the room. Groups should not be symmetrical but some form of balance should prevail, with either vertical or horizontal lines forming the basis for the grouping. The experienced eye can tell if it is the tops of the frames that would look better lined up, or the outer edges or whether the group should be centred and symmetrical. A useful tip is to lay the pictures out on the floor to get an idea of the overall look. Having decided on the layout, it is important to keep the gaps between the individual pictures consistent.

THE PRACTICALITIES OF HANGING

It is difficult to hang pictures, especially groups of pictures, by yourself, unless you have an experienced eye and have measured and marked out the wall with military precision. Making a mistake with the position of a picture hook can lead to a devastating mess of unwanted holes and flaking plaster. It is advisable to have someone hold up the picture for you before committing yourself to the hammer so that you can stand back and judge the balance of your grouping from a distance.

When measuring where to place the picture hook, first pull the picture wire or cord up in the centre with the picture hook and measure the distance between the top of the frame and the base of the hook. Then measure down from the ceiling or the base of the cornice (assuming that the ceiling line is level) to the point where you want the top of the frame to be. Then add on the measurement you have just taken from the back of the picture (top of frame to base of hook) and mark the wall with a soft carpenter's pencil (the kind that rubs out easily without damaging paint or wallpaper). Remember always to measure to the base of the hook, as the wire or cord will hang from the hook, not the nail – it's an obvious point, but all-too-often overlooked.

For large, heavy pictures it is advisable to get expert help as the walls will require drilling and plugging and checking that the painting is level can be an onerous task. Heavy paintings should be hung from two hooks or suspended from a picture rail on two lengths of brass chain.

FRAMING

The choice of frame will depend very much on the subject matter, the type of artwork, its style and its age. Frames and mounts should be chosen to enhance not distract, to complement but not dominate. That said, framing is by and large a question of personal choice.

OIL PAINTINGS

Traditional oil paintings look best in traditional frames. Antique frames were hand-carved and thought of as an integral part of the whole composition. In the early Renaissance, designs for frames were taken from architectural features often found in churches, which were the art galleries of the time. Off-the-peg frames came into their own around the sixteenth century when artists were producing more individual paintings rather than working alongside architects on frescoes. At this time frame-making became a separate trade for craftsmen, who were often more interested in displaying their skills for the ornate than in matching a frame to an artwork. Antique frames are works of art in themselves and are priced accordingly, so if the original frame has been separated from the picture or damaged beyond repair, you may be shocked at the price of purchasing an antique replacement. A good reproduction will be a more than adequate substitute.

Reproduction frames can be made up to your own specification and finished in a number of ways. The most popular and suitable finish for traditional frames is gilding. It is expensive but it looks it and it is certainly well worthwhile employing an expert to finish reproduction frames or carry out any repairs to antique ones.

The advantage of gilding is that it requires very little

RIGHT *An unusual European portrait of an Indian prince or maharajah. The frame with its lovely patina of age was very probably the original choice of the artist. Frame and picture are very well-matched.*

cleaning and it ages gracefully with little more attention that the occasional flick of the duster. Water gilding is the most expensive and gives the finest finish. It is achieved by applying real gold leaf onto a base of gesso and bole which is then burnished to give a wonderful depth of colour and patina of age. Next on the scale comes oil gilding, a simpler process which produces a more matt appearance without much depth of colour. A cheaper substitute is gilding powder, which is good for touching up worn patches (it can be stained to match colour) or for picking out certain mouldings on a frame.

Other traditional finishes include staining, waxing and polishing. Natural wood grains can be enhanced by staining and then sealing with a French polish or shellac finish. Decorative paint finishes, such as antiquing or crackle glazing can give the wood an aged look, and hardwood frames can look very attractive with a gilded slip set against the oil painting to set it off.

Oil paintings do not normally require glass as their surfaces are already sealed with varnish. Because they are naturally bolder in appearance than watercolours or prints, they can take stronger frames. Even small oils can be greatly enhanced by a bold, albeit simple, frame. The important thing to remember is not to let the frame distract from the painting.

WATERCOLOURS

The traditional treatment for watercolours is a bland, neutral-coloured mount and a plain gilt or wooden frame. Personally I prefer a mount with a few simple washlines using colour picked out from the painting. The mounts themselves should not be mean in size, and the smaller the subject the larger the mount should be. Artists frequently leave irregular unpainted areas around the edges of their work, so it is sometimes necessary to use the mount to crop part of the picture or alternatively to expose a uniform space all the way round. Coloured mounts can look good on black and white engravings or monotone subjects but on delicate, subtle watercolours they can detract.

For older, traditional watercolours I prefer to bow to convention with a simple gilt or natural wood frame or a combination of the two. Bolder, contemporary subjects, however, need a bolder approach – perhaps a metal frame or one with a painted finish – that blends in with the room's decorative style.

ANTIQUE PRINTS

Genuine old prints require a sympathetic approach as anything too loud will detract from their quality. Antique prints often originated from early illustrated books. Many such books were printed for the benefit of architects and builders, and the subject matter was consequently architectural, from plans and façades to beautifully detailed door mouldings and accessories. Other popular subjects were maps sketched by explorers back from their travels, or flora and fauna catalogued by botanists and scientists on their fact-finding missions to far-flung corners of the globe.

Print-collecting is made more interesting if you can recognize the different printing techniques. The earliest prints were cut, like the earliest type, from blocks of wood. These are necessarily small in size, with thick, bold lines. Much later, artists learned to cut from the endgrain of very dense woods, such as box, and produced fine and detailed work, but again small in scale. These are known a relief prints.

With the advent of engraving on copper and steel, larger images could be produced with far greater detail and delicacy. To achieve tones of grey, mezzotint (where the surface is covered with minute indentations) was developed. These prints from metal, together with etchings and aquatints (where the lines are bitten into the

LEFT *A modern abstract painting for which the artist clearly did not intend a frame.*

RIGHT *A modern abstract, simply framed, provides a foil to a 17th century chair and an early oak chest.*

metal plate with acid) are known as intaglio prints.

The third group of prints are surface prints, such as lithographs, screen prints and those produced by mechanical processes such as chromolithography. These are the only types of colour print, with the other techniques colour will have been added by hand (often recently).

All these different printing methods produce a distinctive edge to the print, so when framing original prints be sure to leave the edges of the paper showing. If there is a title it can either be included within the print or displayed in a separate box cut out of the mount.

MODERN PRINTS
In the framing of modern or reproduction prints you can really get creative. The mounts can be enhanced with

ABOVE *The ship print in its simple but elegant gilt wood and black painted frame is flanked by drawings and pen and wash studies. Mounts for old prints should be kept simple.*

decorative lines, borders of marbled paper, double mounts of differing colours and no end of corner treatments or stencilled designs.

Experiment with different frames, not only colours and finishes, but shapes: circles, ovals and hexagons. The shape of the print does not have to determine the shape of the frame and mount, and different combinations will only add interest. Frames can be finished to tie in with a particular colour scheme or with the print itself, but do beware of killing off the prints with clashing or overwhelming colours.

CARE AND REPAIR

Oil paintings will naturally deteriorate with age and will eventually require some sort of restoration. However with considerate conservation, you can minimize damage and prolong their life. Conservation begins with choosing a sensible location for the painting to hang, away from direct sunlight and sources of heat. Over-dry conditions will cause cracking, a damp atmosphere will encourage mould growth, and rapid changes of temperature may cause the wooden stretchers to crack or warp.

CHECKING FOR DAMAGE

The instantly recognizable signs of deterioration in an oil painting are large, flaking cracks which have curled at the edges, and an uneven look to the surface of the painting. Small surface cracks are part of the natural ageing process and do not signal a potential problem.

Study the back of the painting as well as the front. Look for water stains which may only be visible on the reverse of the canvas and check for an accumulation of dust between the stretchers. Hold the painting up to a light and you may discover small holes and cracks that are not so easily seen from the front. Experts use a range of sophisticated techniques to assess damage but the earlier any damage is spotted, the less harm done. Oil paintings of any value should always be cleaned and restored by an expert. Unless you have considerable knowledge of the subject, even simple cleaning can cause harm.

VARNISHING

To protect an oil painting from dust, smoke and daily life, a restorer will apply a coat of special picture varnish. These varnishes can be removed without damaging the paint itself and then re-applied after cleaning. They will protect the painting, enhance the colour and give the surface a consistent patina. New varnish should never be applied over an existing dirty varnish as the build-up will change the colour and the nature of the original work.

WATERCOLOURS AND PRINTS

Like all pictures, watercolours and prints will deteriorate with excess light and humidity. Much of the earlier paper used contained chemicals that reacted badly to the environment and deteriorated quickly. Today acid-free paper and mounting boards are widely used, guaranteeing a longer life.

If you are restoring an old print or watercolour, it is important to ask your framer to use acid-free mounts and boards. If you wish to preserve an original mount, then ensure it is lined with a new acid-free board.

Typical of the damage to artwork on paper is 'foxing' – brownish-yellow spots caused by damp and fungal growth. These can easily be removed by an expert using a special form of bleach. Another common blemish is acid burn, caused by too much light and acidity in the paper. It creates a yellow/brown discoloration of the paper (as seen in old newspapers) and also causes a dry brittleness which could well result in the paper cracking.

To conserve your prints and watercolours, keep them well away from light and damp. Light causes all sorts of damage to paper and artwork so watercolours and prints should be displayed well away from sunlight. Glass will protect them from dust and grime, but not from ultra-violet radiation unless the glass is specifically designed for that task.

Valuable prints should not be hung in kitchens or bathrooms, as damp will cause damage however well-sealed the frame. You can minimize damage from damp penetration by allowing air to circulate right around a picture, perhaps by inserting a wedge of cork between the picture and the wall.

BELOW *A treasure trove of prints, some hung from bars hooked onto the picture rail, some on easels and some awaiting perusal in a print stand.*

MIRRORS AND SPACE

One of the most effective ways of creating space and light in a room which lacks these qualities is to use mirror glass – and plenty of it. In bathrooms, where mirrors perform very functional tasks, entire walls can look wonderful mirrored from top to bottom. Mirrors enable you to bring sparkle to dark alcoves and even to ceilings. They can alter proportions by creating illusions of depth, bring light to dark hallways and widen narrow passages.

New mirror glass can appear modern and harsh and may look quite out of place in a classical interior. You can overcome this problem by using sheets of tinted or antiqued glass, available from specialist suppliers, framed with wooden mouldings to soften the edges.

LEFT *An ingenious way to enjoy the back of this classical stone sculpture and to enhance the perfect proportions of a gracious room. Antique mirror glass is easy on the eye.*

BELOW *Clever folding screens made of painted bamboo and panels of mirror glass bounce light and sparkle all around the room and double the impact of treasured collections.*

ABOVE A long, narrow room with windows on only one side is given an extra dimension by this huge antique gilt mirror which looks like an archway opening into another room. Heavy mirrors require chains and strong fixing bolts.

LEFT A lovely mirror with an oriental-style gilt and enamel frame is hung on a wall of antiqued mirror glass panels – glass on glass. The effect on this tiny room is quite magical. The indoor palms are reflected over and over again to create the illusion of an opulent, palm-fronded Arabian palace.

RIGHT A magnificent mirror and its matching gilt and marble console table have their impact doubled thanks to the simple mirror glass panels set into the surrounding walls.

ABOVE *An interesting way to show off a picture. This one has been hung on top of a mirror glass panel with a custom-built frame around it. The hook is concealed with a bow.*

LEFT *These magnificently ornate 18th century mirrors with candle sconces at the base, take the place of paintings either side of an elaborately gilded doorway.*

BELOW *A delightful cosy corner of a Victorian room gets a glow of warmth from the fireplace and added sparkle from two pretty little decorative mirrors.*

DECORATIVE MIRRORS

As with picture frames, mirrors are available in a variety of styles and shapes from the simple and restrained to the over-blown baroque. If you cannot find the decorative mirror you are looking for, then it is perfectly possible to create your own design. You can either buy an antique frame and have old glass inserted into it, or you can first find your piece of glass and have a frame made to suit.

Decorative mirrors can look marvellous in any room, but they look particularly attractive when reflecting

ABOVE *A brand new piece of mirror glass has been given an eccentric topping of sculpted fruit and flowers. The glass panels run down the sides of the fireplace, so it seems disconnected from the wall and appears to float in space.*

candlelight, which makes them a natural for dining areas. In sitting rooms a magnificent mirror can act as a focal point in place of a painting while smaller mirrors can be used here and there around the walls to balance and control the fall of natural and artificial light.

RIGHT *Gilt wood ornamented with flamboyant rococo scrollwork and rocaille framing an early piece of mirror glass. Old mirror like this was produced with an amalgam of silver and mercury, and exposure to damp makes it go grey and patchy. However these imperfections of age are to be treasured and on no account exchanged for modern glass.*

BELOW *In this little hall-cum-dining room, a corner cupboard has been given a mirrored door made from two old pieces of mirror glass in bad condition, but the imperfections of the glass give a softer and more flattering reflection. The frame is probably made up from some old gilded sections and some new ones to complete the illusion.*

ABOVE *A flamboyant Art Deco dressing table mirror has a bright silvered finish enhanced with lines cut into the back of the glass. Coloured mirror glass, used here for the panels running down the sides, was very popular during the period. Peach and apple green were the most favoured shades.*

COLLECTIONS

THERE IS A COLLECTOR HIDING INSIDE EVERY ONE OF US, WHETHER IT
BE OF TIN SOLDIERS OR TENNIS TROPHIES, GLASS DECANTERS, OLD
GARDENING TOOLS OR CHINESE GINGER JARS. COLLECTIONS TELL US
A LOT ABOUT PEOPLE, ABOUT THEIR PASSIONS AND THEIR STYLES, AND
THEY BRING AN INSTANT TOUCH OF PERSONALITY TO ANY ROOM.

CERAMICS

The word ceramics is derived from the Greek *keramos*, meaning clay. It embraces all forms of pottery and porcelain from humble earthenware teapots to priceless Ming dynasty vases. A ceramics collection of some kind is therefore within everyone's reach, and a hunt around most households will yield more ceramic objects than practically anything else.

Collections, of course, have to be focused but that certainly does not mean that the items have to be expensive. By reading up-to-date specialist publications or talking to experts, it is possible to acquire a working knowledge of a limited area of ceramics, so you can judge for yourself the fairness of the asking price and the quality of the pieces you are after.

Half the fun of building up a collection is the challenge of gradually hunting down bargain pieces. Do not expect to build up a collection overnight. By finding out about your subject and taking your time you will be more likely to end up with a well-planned group.

PORCELAIN AND POTTERY

Pottery is the term generally used to describe all forms of ceramics other than porcelain. The most common types

LEFT *A collection of old ceramic vessels in the Ancient Chinese style, chosen for their form and finish, and displayed in a suitably rustic environment.*

BELOW *A pair of English soft-paste porcelain gravy boats and a chinoiserie bowl dating from the 18th century. Also in period are the tapestry wall hanging and the portrait.*

ABOVE *Shelves laden with porcelain in the Sèvres style with its characteristic palette of pea-green and pink. This design is called* rose pompadour.

of pottery are stoneware, made from a fine grey clay that fires to a hard, non-porous finish, and earthenware, a coarser clay that requires a baked-on glaze to render it non-porous.

Porcelain differs from pottery in both appearance and texture. It is made from a fine white pure clay and when baked it is translucent when held up to the light. True porcelain, or hard-paste porcelain as it is more commonly known, originated in China over 1000 years ago. The Europeans struggled to come up with a copy of this unique quality product, and their early attempts resulted in soft-paste porcelain made from a formula of white clay and 'frit' (used to make glass) to give the necessary translucency. Telling the difference between the two is

LEFT *Blue and white Chinese porcelain displayed on and below a hall table on a sunny yellow-painted landing. These pieces are a mixture of real Chinese porcelain and copies from European factories.*

BELOW *The top shelf of a radiator cover holds a massed collection of ancient Chinese tea-caddies shaped like little ceramic bricks, each with a unique design.*

hard on simple white-glazed plates and bowls but the soft-paste porcelains do not lend themselves to the fine detailing and the clear bright colours and glazes that are the hallmark of true porcelain.

CHOOSING A CATEGORY

A particular passion may already have you in its grip, be it the work of a certain artist like the British designer Clarice Cliff whose *Art Deco* creations are so sought after, curiosities such as cow-shaped cream jugs, or a particular type of china such as tin-glazed earthenware. How and what you collect is up to you and your taste. Perhaps the easiest way to start is by collecting by colour and/or item, such as green jugs, German drinking vessels or white candlesticks. Another route is to collect different items decorated with the same theme whether it be birds or hot-air balloons.

Tens of thousands of beautifully proportioned blue and white Chinese porcelain vases, bowls and plates were exported from China as ballast aboard the vessels of the East India Trading Companies, and these have always been thought of as a safe buy as, indeed, have unmarked English blue and white porcelains. These are certainly a better bet for the novice collector than coloured wares which have attracted the attention of fakers since the beginning of the nineteenth century.

Collecting is definitely more fun if you choose something that is not easy to come by. This does not mean the items have to be rare or expensive, just unusual, quirky or different.

DISPLAYING CERAMICS

Every piece deserves to be displayed to its best advantage. I have many one-off individual pieces, each with its own story and attached memories, that stand alone, combined perhaps with silver, glass or books on a shelf. On the other hand, a unique collection of one type of ceramics, for example a pretty assortment of enamelled

BELOW *It was the cobalt-blue underglaze of Chinese porcelain that was so prized and imitated. Some pieces follow traditional shapes, others were specially made for the European market.*

porcelain boxes, will look better displayed as a collection and not mixed with other porcelain.

Eye-level is another important consideration. Little boxes with beautiful lids obviously need to be displayed on a low shelf or table so the detail can be better admired. Large bowls, jars and vases may well look better at floor level, so consider grouping big bold items under a console or side table where they will not risk getting knocked over.

Plates can be hung on walls using special metal hanging brackets that expand to fit any size of plate. They look good in groups or even intermingled with pictures. They can look equally effective on dressers or behind glass in display cabinets as long as they are well lit. I often use wooden plate stands to display a pair of particularly beautiful dishes or plates on a table with other items.

ABOVE *This is just a small part of my collection of enamel boxes. Some of them are very old but most are modern. Boxes such as these were first made (especially in Staffordshire, England and in London's Battersea) at the end of the 18th century as a cheaper alternative to the delicate porcelain originals from the great factories such as Meissen. The pair of urn-shaped vases are of English porcelain, made at the turn of the 19th century when the gilding process produced a much softer yellow than later in the century.*

LEFT *A collection of white ceramics in use at the dinner table. The fine white porcelain plates have just a touch of gilding at the rim and the white theme is taken up by the figurines used as centrepieces. On the mantle piece is a collection of painted Staffordshire pottery figures.*

LEFT *The ever-popular Chinese porcelain, this time massed on top of a cupboard and interspersed with coloured, enamelled Chinese figures. Chinese blue and white porcelain first became the rage in the reign of William and Mary (1689–1702). It was so popular that some pieces of furniture were specially designed to display the pieces effectively.*

BELOW *An eclectic collection of blue and white china that goes beyond the Chinese to include Victorian and Edwardian patterns and even finds place for the simple, utilitarian English 20th century blue-striped kitchenware by T G Green.*

CARE AND REPAIR

Most porcelain and pottery can be washed in warm water with a mild detergent, but do not immerse repaired pieces as this will weaken the adhesive. Just dip them in quickly and wipe them over. For very delicate and valuable pieces, line the sink with soft towels or rubber pads and wash only one piece at a time. Use a fine brush to ease away the dirt from intricate crevices, as a cloth may catch on delicate protrusions.

Let the pieces dry on a cloth or paper towel and, if necessary, give them a final wipe once dry. Handle the pieces individually and do not stack them. If they have to be stacked for storage, line the pieces with tissue paper. Never pick up items by handles or spouts that have been weakened by repairs and watch out for loose bits such as lids. Everyday dusting should be done with care, using a soft duster or an artist's brush which will help you get the dust out of crevices and indicate decorative flourishes.

One final word of warning: if ceramic objects are displayed on a polished surface, it is a good idea to cover the bottoms with small pieces of felt to stop them moving. Even small vibrations can cause porcelain to move on a polished mahogany sideboard.

GLASS

Rare and beautiful glassware makes a stunning-looking collection, but even everyday items can add sparkle to a room. Wine glasses, goblets, tumblers, platters, candlesticks and bowls need not be hidden behind cupboard doors when not in use — display them on shelves, dressers or sideboards and enjoy the way the light gleams and bounces off the surfaces.

A BRIEF HISTORY OF GLASS

Venice dominated the glass-making industry from the thirteenth century to the late eighteenth century. Elsewhere in Europe glassware was considered an expensive luxury as it was invariably imported from Italy. From the late eighteenth century onward, England and Ireland excelled in glass making, particularly in the manufacture of richly coloured glass and bright, clear lead glass which could be cut or faceted like a diamond. During the early Georgian era, hand-blown glass, as opposed to moulded glass, resulted in more delicate work. The development of engraving, etching and enamelling techniques also helped to produced some fine, intricate glassware.

Throughout the Victorian era, glass products continued to develop and the mechanization of the industry led to new techniques such as acid etching, which was both cheaper and quicker than the scratch engraving or copper wheel engraving techniques used by craftsmen of earlier periods. Much glassware since the nineteenth century has been produced by the press mould method which originated in America as a way of manufacturing a product that closely resembles hand-cut glass.

Glass, if handled with care, can be very resistant to age which makes it difficult to work out the exact age of a piece. It was rare for glass to be marked and frequently the most reliable way of telling the age is by the design and style of the object — punch bowls and toasting glasses, for instance, are typically Georgian pieces, cut glass was a rare technique before 1760, and etched glass is very typical of the Victorian era. Genuine hand-blown glass will be slightly uneven and asymmetrical in shape.

COLLECTOR'S GLASS

A little knowledge is essential before embarking on the sale rooms, antique shops and street markets in search of collectable glass, especially as its provenance is often so hard to establish. As with any collection, it is important to be guided by what you like rather than get carried away with historical detail, otherwise your collection may end up as a dull if accurate catalogue rather than an inspired still life.

DECANTERS

Until 1860 and the introduction of the labelled bottle, wine was purchased in wooden casks or simple coloured storage bottles and it was therefore essential to decant wine in order to serve it at table. Hence the glass

LEFT *A table sparkling with blue and clear glass goblets. Blue glass was first made by an important group of glass makers centred on Bristol, England, in the 18th century, and has since been known as Bristol blue glass, even though it is now made elsewhere.*

RIGHT *A matching set of pressed-glass jugs. Press-moulding was a 19th century factory process intended to simulate hand-cut glass. The first patent for the process was taken out by an American factory in 1825 for the manufacture of glass furniture knobs.*

LEFT *A silver tray full of elegant Victorian stoppered decanters and a claret jug with silver mounts. Just visible are two silver wine labels which were made from about 1725 until around 1860, when paper labels on wine bottles were required by law. Silver wine labels described the type of wine, such as 'Madeira', or 'Sherry'.*

RIGHT *A wonderful table setting glistening with glass and candlelight set off by the glow of polished mahogany. The mass of garden flowers are the main source of colour here and the table looks both welcoming and elegant.*

decanter, a most elegant addition to a formal table setting, a bar or drinks tray.

The first decanters tended to be heavy in style and stopperless, as it was normal for the contents to be consumed during the meal. Stoppers were introduced when port became a popular drink. Early Georgian decanters are generally of clear glass with simple cut-glass decoration or engraving. Mid-eighteenth-century decanters were club- or mallet-shaped with tall, narrow necks and often a spire-shaped stopper. Later designs became wider at the base with shorter necks and a flat lip to prevent dripping, and the stopper became more rounded. It was these bell-shaped ship's decanters and the square spirit decanters that evolved throughout the Georgian and Regency period that set the trend for the styles still used today. Victorian claret jugs were elaborately cut and coloured and were frequently decorated with silver collars, mounted hinged lids, and silver or glass handles.

When buying an old decanter, make sure the stopper is original. It should fit correctly, the decoration should match that on the decanter and, unless it has been deliberately ground down, it will invariably be chipped.

JUGS, GLASSES AND VASES

I often use glass jugs as flower vases so they get a chance to be seen and used. Old jugs, clear or coloured, cut or engraved, enamelled or cameo, were generally made to serve home-made cordials or water and so can sometimes be found with a set of matching glasses, but complete sets are difficult to find.

Antique glasses, or special bowls such as syllabub or jelly glasses used for desserts in the eighteenth century, make good collections as well as useful containers for small floral arrangements. Victorian glass vases are particularly rich in colour and decoration. Cameo glass was extremely popular at the time. It was made of different layers of coloured glass etched or carved away to reveal the colours below. These heavily decorated pieces are an

LEFT Coloured glass was popular for scent bottles because the very earliest bottles, dating from the 13th century, were made to simulate semi-precious stones such as agate.

acquired taste and personally I find them difficult to use with other pieces as their richness tends to overwhelm.

If you intend to mix glass vases with porcelain, perhaps on a dinner table, clear glass, with the colour coming from the flowers, will always look the most elegant.

SCENT BOTTLES

Scent became popular in the eighteenth century and, like wine and spirits, it was necessary to decant it into attractive containers for day-to-day use. Most scent bottles were made from glass with silver or gilt tops, sometimes with precious or semi-precious stones set into the lid. Jewellers and goldsmiths were often involved in the design of holders for portable scent bottles and later, when scent was actually sold in small decorative bottles,

ABOVE *The distinctive look of* Art Deco *glass by French glass makers Lalique and Gallé, who blazed a trail in the making of stylish glass objects.*

perfume houses commissioned famous glass makers such as the famous French manufacturers Lalique and Gallé to design bottles specially for them.

Venetian coloured scent bottles are popular with collectors, as are bottles of blue Bristol glass and bottles known as *sulphides* which have ceramic medallions incorporated into the glass.

PAPERWEIGHTS

Collecting paperweights can be a fascinating, if expensive hobby. Glass paperweights were originally made in France from about 1840, and French makers have continued to dominate the market, creating the most intricate and refined designs. It was they who perfected the art of *millefiori*, achieved by placing differently coloured glass rods together, heating them and then cutting through to form intricate multi-coloured canes. Plant and animal motifs are made by sculpting glass over heat and then setting the resulting piece in a dome of clear glass to seal and magnify.

The best French paperweights come from the Baccarat, Saint Louis and Clichy factories. Sometimes, but unfortunately not always, these factories would identify their wares with initials or by repeating a motif. The Baccarat factory, for example would often cut a star motif into the base or use star-shaped canes.

Today, paperweights are in great demand and are made in Britain, France, Italy and America, some factories producing limited editions for collectors. Be careful with paperweights: they may look and feel robust but they are all too easily damaged. Mint condition antique paperweights are expensive items, a few original scratches will reduce their value dramatically, but paperweights that have been ground down to remove defects are less valuable still.

CANDLESTICKS

In my view, beautiful glass candlesticks do more to enhance a dining table than silver ones. Alive with glowing candles, they dazzle, reflecting the light and making the whole table glisten invitingly.

Early glass candleholders were quite practical in design, and it is the simpler single candlesticks that have survived best, as the branched holders or candelabra were all too easily damaged. Most of the elaborate pieces with cut-glass lustres date from the mid-eighteenth century. They were intended for sideboards, rather than tables, and were often placed in front of mirrors to reflect the light into the room.

BELOW *The red decanter is an example of 'flashing', a technique involving an outer layer of coloured glass which is then cut through to produce a pattern.*

ABOVE *A pair of elaborate cameo glass candlesticks with dangling lustres to catch the light. They have been placed either side of a Venetian mirror in a formal, symmetrical arrangement perfectly suited to their style.*

LEFT *An assortment of candlesticks, posy vases, jugs and a salt cellar made of press-moulded glass are teamed up with lustrous shells and a silver candle snuffer.*

CARE AND REPAIR

Glass is a delicate material and needs to be handled with care and treated with respect. Never put good, old or delicate glass in a dishwasher. Wash pieces individually with warm water and a mild detergent and rinse the soap off well. I like to let glass dry on its own, preferably on a cloth or towel, and then give it a final wipe with a soft, dry cotton cloth. Do not wash repaired glass as this may dissolve the glue; just wipe or dust. Do not stack glass: if it has to be stored, keep the pieces in a dust-free environment with space between them. Chipped, cracked or broken glass should be dealt with by an expert and the same applies to stains, as harsh detergents or bleaches in untrained hands could create even more damage.

SILVER

Silver is a magnificently malleable material. It can be rolled, hammered, etched, sawn, enamelled, engraved, cast and even drawn out into filigree threads. It can be melted down and re-worked into a more 'modern' style (the fate of many magnificent old pieces) and it has been seen as a good investment, as it could always be pawned, sold off or melted down into coinage when times were bad.

STERLING SILVER AND PLATE

Pure silver is too soft to be made into articles for everyday use and so it is alloyed, or mixed, with another metal to strengthen it. The most commonly used is copper, the addition of which leaves the appearance of silver unchanged. The standard mix, classified as sterling silver, is 92.5 percent pure silver to 7.5 percent base metal.

The demand for cheaper silver led to the introduction of plate, which is made by fusing a thin coating of sterling silver onto a metal, usually copper, base.

Hallmarks are intended as a guide to the purity of the silver and the provenance of the piece, and to the serious

LEFT *A classic 19th century American table setting at Homewood House in Baltimore with an elaborate three-arm candelabra and elegant serving dishes and coasters.*

BELOW *Silver chafing dishes had an inner dish which rested on a trivet so there was a space beneath the hot food to pour boiling water, thus keeping the food warmer for longer.*

ABOVE A collection of well-cared-for silver objects. The tall boxes at the back of the table are tea caddies, there are sugar tongs and lorgnettes, snuff boxes and silver beakers.

collector of silver they repay study but, like many things in life, they cannot be relied upon. Hallmarks may be forged or the piece may have been reworked, so it is unsafe to judge a piece on its hallmark alone. Take your instincts into account, look at the quality of the work, the weight of the piece, the style, design and decoration, then if it pleases you and the price is right, buy it, look after it well and enjoy it.

DECORATED SILVER

Chasing was a form of decoration used on sheet metal and cast silver items. Designs were hammered into the silver from the front and seen in reverse from the back or the inside. Embossing uses the reverse technique, working from the inside or back to produce raised patterns. *Repoussé* work is a combination of the two, working from both front and back, resulting in greater relief. Die-casting is the most economical form of chasing. It involves stamping out designs on a press, and it was much used for popular mass-produced items in Victorian times.

Pierced decoration was originally carried out with a

tiny hammer and chisel and subsequently with fine hand saws or mechanical punches, and is to be found on smaller decorative pieces such as baskets or salt cellars. Cut-card work refers to soldering shapes cut from sheet silver, and was used both as a form of decoration and as a way of strengthening joints between handles and spouts on tea and coffee pots. Gilding was used on elaborate pieces used for display rather than everyday use, except in the case of saltcellars and jugs where it was used as a lining to protect the silver against corrosion.

DRINKING, SMOKING AND BUTTONING UP

Most collections start because items of special history and personal value have been passed from generation to generation and added to along the way. Drink-related silverware is fun to collect and ranges from corkscrews, decanter labels, wine funnels and spirit flasks to the ladles, fruit strainers and nutmeg graters associated with the Georgian punch habit.

The tobacco habit also produced a wealth of collectibles. Tobacco jars and snuff boxes were made as far back as the early 1600's. Early examples tend to the simple and plain but they got more and more ornate as time went by. Cigar and cigarette boxes and matchbox cases can make for a good-looking if not very health-conscious collection. Dress accessories can make a good collection too. Buttons, button hooks, buckles and belts were often beautifully crafted, particularly buckles, which were a highly-prized fashion item in the eighteenth century.

SILVER TABLEWARE

There is nothing more inviting than a dining table laid with beautiful porcelain, glass and silver, complete with

BELOW A small grouping of silver thimbles, propelling pencils, a cut-glass scent bottle, a pocket watch and a charming rattle with silver bells for a very privileged baby.

ABOVE *Simple silver candlesticks and coasters decorate a table set with beautiful silver flatware in a classic pattern. Such patterns were made by several different silversmiths.*

flowers and soft candlelight. Silver, with its soft glow, is a vital component of the magic.

Cutlery and canteens of flatware vary considerably in design, age and quality. Complete original antique sets are difficult to find and expensive when you do, so it is often more realistic to build a set of the same pattern by different makers. Original knives are particularly difficult to come by as they sustained more damage than forks and spoons. Often it is necessary to buy new knives to complete an old set.

Antique silver dishes and platters were usually designed for table use and were therefore practical and simple. Pieces designed purely for decoration, such as centrepieces, were usually elaborately decorated and sometimes gilded. But it is the smaller items that can do so much to enhance a table: baskets, cruets, napkin rings and small vases were often beautifully worked and intricately decorated. Claret jugs are, in my view, one of the most attractive table accessories you can find, their elegant shapes combining the sparkle of glass with the enrichment of silver.

Silver candlesticks can take their place not only on the dining table but elsewhere in the house on mantelpieces, dressing tables and sideboards. The range, of course, is

LEFT *In Victorian times, dressing table sets came with fitted boxes for travelling, but today it is unlikely you would want to move them far from home. This tortoiseshell and silver set is one of my prized possessions. I think it looks at its best laid out on a crisp white embroidered cloth on a polished mahogany surface.*

BELOW *A restrained silver-gilt dressing table set dating from the 1920's or 30's. It has little decoration except for the elegant silver MS monogram. The circular box was used for loose powder and such boxes often came with a huge silk powder puff that just fitted inside the box.*

enormous, from elaborate three-arm candelabra to simple fluted stems, not forgetting the work of contemporary silversmiths, some of whom are producing modern designs every bit as stunning as any antique.

DRESSING TABLE ACCESSORIES

One of my prized possessions is my collection of silver and tortoiseshell dressing table accessories. I have brush and comb sets, bottles, jars and pots which make a magnificent display. Silver and glass scent bottles and powder boxes look attractive too, especially when combined with silver-framed photographs.

Many antique dressing table sets, especially Victorian ones, were originally boxed for travelling. Today many of these complete sets have been split up as the boxes have disintegrated, but a variety of styles often looks more attractive than a matching set.

DESK EQUIPMENT

Silver photograph frames are a particular love of mine: I don't think you can ever have enough of them. They can do more to personalize a room than anything else, and they can be moved around to create different areas of interest. Silver magnifying glasses, letter openers, card holders, seals, blotters and ink wells might not be particularly useful desk accessories in today's computerized world, but these small items sell at reasonable prices, they hold their value well and do more for the look of a desk or library table than a sea of black leather accessories and a battery of solar-powered gadgetry.

RIGHT *A sparkle of silver can really lighten up any corner of any room. This is a pretty collection of little silver frames, a salt cellar and a couple of card cases.*

BELOW *Silver looks right in any setting. It looks grand on polished wood, it glints and gleams on starched white linen and here it looks warm and rich on a dark paisley cloth.*

COPPER, PEWTER AND BRASS

Athough lacking in the finesse of silver, brass, pewter and copper have been used to make some useful and very decorative products. Copper was often used for domestic household products such as warming pans, saucepans and jelly moulds, although when used for cooking the utensils were lined with tin to prevent contamination. Today copper kitchenware is mainly decorative as it takes many hours of polishing to maintain copper's rich lustre. There is no doubt that, given the right setting, the odd copper pot hanging from a kitchen ceiling can add character to the room, especially when intermingled with other decorative items.

Pewter, an alloy of tin and lead was cast into cheap, tough ware, plain in style. Brass, which is an amalgamation of copper and zinc, was said to be the poor man's silver, and consequently some very fine pieces imitating silver designs have been produced, notably candlesticks and canisters, trays and ashtrays. Today brass is widely

ABOVE *An interesting collection of multifaceted brass containers and some decorated dressing table boxes that are probably imitations of designs for similar silver items.*

LEFT *A full collection of copper pans and copper and brass kitchen utensils make a very impressive display but that comforting glow represents a lot of elbow grease. If you can be bothered with the cleaning problems, copper pans are wonderful to cook with, as copper transfers heat more quickly than any other metal, but they need to be lined with tin or silver to prevent dangerous chemical reactions between heat and food. The one piece that is an essential for all serious cooks is an unlined copper bowl for whisking egg whites. For some reason, egg whites whipped in copper rise and foam spectacularly.*

used throughout the home in light fittings, bathroom fittings, door furniture and fireside accessories. Fire irons and firedogs were, and still are, made in a combination of metals. It is always best to keep to one style, so if your fire basket is made of steel with brass decorations, stick to that same combination for the fire irons, firedogs and fender.

CARE OF METALS

Silver will tarnish when exposed to air because of the sulphur in the atmosphere. When not in use, keep individual silver pieces sealed in plastic bags. For everyday cleaning, silver can be washed in warm, soapy water (do not use a strong detergent). Dry at once with a cloth to avoid drying marks. For more thorough cleaning use special silver foam applied with a damp sponge and once dry, polish with a soft cloth. Silver dips are useful for small items that are difficult to clean, but do not use too frequently or let them soak for too long as it may weaken the metal. Do not over-polish antique silver as you may remove its natural ageing patina. Ensure salt cellars are used with liners as the salt will attack the metal. Never use abrasive cleaners on silver and do not immerse items with wooden handles or felt-covered bases.

Brass and copper items should be treated in the same way, using cleaning materials specially formulated for that particular metal.

ABOVE *Pewter was made in Europe from Roman times by alloying brittle tin with more malleable copper or lead. Pewter is a soft metal, easily dented and scratched, but it burnishes to a lovely sheen.*

BELOW *American 19th century* tôle-ware. Tôle *is japanned or painted tinware originating in France in the 1740's.*

BELOW *Pewter has been used for domestic items since the 14th century. It went out of fashion in Europe with the advent of silver plate, but has remained a firm favourite in America.*

SCULPTURE

Ever since the Renaissance, sculptures, especially bronzes and marble, have been popular with collectors. Bronze figures are generally better suited to the domestic interior, as marble busts and figures tend to be on the massive side, but there is nothing more spectacular than to enter a spacious hallway where a stunning marble bust is displayed on a marble table top or to come across a wonderful nude sculpture languishing on a stone or marble floor. Sadly such scenarios are rarely possible today.

Unless you have your eye on a delightful Degas or a massive Moore, bronzes are still a relatively inexpensive art form. Casts of animals and human poses can often be found in antique shops. They tend to be copies of originals depicting heroes and romantic figures and, because of the large quantities of casts that have been produced

BELOW *A group of sculptural fragments of stone, marble and bonded resin. The standing nude is an anatomical figure showing the musculature of the male body.*

ABOVE *A pretty marble bust in the 18th century French classical style. Her impact would be much diminished if she were surrounded by a sea of trinkets.*

from the same moulds over the years, it is often difficult to tell their exact age. I find the subject matter of the bronze almost irrelevant: modern or traditional, animal or human, a well-detailed bronze with a rich patina looks wonderful in any setting, and it does not need to form part of an expensive collection.

Figures made from spelter and cast iron were made as a cheaper substitute for bronze, especially around the *Art Nouveau* and *Art Deco* periods. They can look equally stunning, yet the detail is not so fine and they do not age well as they become brittle.

CARE OF BRONZE AND MARBLE

The dark brown or greenish patina which builds up on bronze figures adds character and value to the piece and should not be removed with cleaning.

Most bronzes and marble sculptures require little more than a light dusting. Dull finishes and a build up of small green surface spots can be removed with a special wax, but any serious marks or mending should be dealt with by an expert.

RIGHT *Three animated Art Deco bronze sculptures displayed in front of a wall of 1920s beaded and tasselled purses. The sculptures, very typical of their time, are unlikely to be one-offs.*

BELOW *A French Empire clock and candlestick set with discreet angelic figures is displayed in the way the maker intended, on a mantelpiece in a formal, symmetrical, classical setting. This combination of bronze with ormolu mounts was very popular during this period. Ormolu is gilded bronze.*

BELOW *A bronze retriever, caught in a typical pose, is the centrepiece of a collection of hunting-related images. An 18th century coloured print of a falconer is propped up behind.*

WOOD

The richness and warmth of wood and its tactile appeal is unlike any other material. If well cared for, that unique finish or patina will improve with age and grow in richness, building up over decades of tender loving care. I find that wood instantly gives a home a cosy atmosphere and a sense of age, whether it comes from a piece of furniture or from architectural details such as a staircase or fireplace.

Wood is essential to the construction of houses and the majority of those used are softwoods that are then painted. Hardwoods and quality softwoods are expensive, which is why we do not have more beautifully panelled libraries or elegant carved staircases. If you are lucky enough to live in an old house which still

BELOW *Amongst the gilt wood frames on this bedroom wall is a touch of whimsy – a lovely piece of gilt wood scrolling foliage, probably a fragment of a much grander frame.*

ABOVE *A collection of old hardwood printing blocks used for hand-blocking fabrics or wallpapers. The lower piece is a carved fragment of a frieze in the Renaissance style.*

possesses some original wooden features, do make the effort to keep them and restore them, in spite of the temptation to rip them out and replace with a more practical but characterless alternative. Stripping paint from old wood is a laborious task and the initial result may not be quite what you expected, but once the room is furnished it is unlikely that your eye will rest on the imperfections, it will rather dwell on the overall ambience and character.

Decorative wooden items are relatively easy to find. There are warehouses and shops that specialize in house clearances and in stripping out old buildings. It is here that I often find old mouldings, curtain poles, banister rails, hand rails and other bits and pieces, some useful today, some useful in the past, some simple yet stylish, others intricately worked and unique in quality, finish and detail.

MOULDINGS AND SCONCES

Old carved mouldings, which may serve no real purpose, can be used very effectively as decorative objects: for instance a pair of mouldings either side of a doorway, or between pictures to break up a straight line. A single wooden swag or bow can look very attractive above a picture or door.

Carved wooden wall sconces range from the plain and undecorated to the gilded and intricately carved. Today there are many good copies of old designs to be found with antiqued finishes so good it is hard to tell them from the real thing. As long as you know what you are buying and the price is set accordingly, then it does not matter if it is genuine or fake. The important thing is the effect you are setting out to achieve.

TREEN

Treen is the name given to a wide range of small, everyday turned and carved items, many of which originated in the seventeenth century. They were considered the poor man's works of art, despite the fact these spoons, bowls, platters and goblets were in use most of the time. These items are very collectible today and look wonderful displayed on dressers and sideboards, or used as fruit

BELOW *A magnificent mahogany door with a swan neck pediment sets the tone for a collection of classical medallions.*

and nut bowls or for holding potpourri. Continental treen is the more elaborate and carved, English pieces tend to be turned and more simple in style, as were American pieces which were often made of fruit wood.

BOXES

Wooden boxes can be found in abundance, made for all sorts of purposes and from all types of wood. The majority were made during the eighteenth and nineteenth centuries as the quality of life improved and the desire grew

ABOVE *The beautifully turned treen urns with marquetry banding are made of fruit wood, the simple bowl in front is probably an English piece.*

to collect things and demonstrate one's wealth to one's neighbours. If you have set your heart on collecting boxes, then it is sensible to pick on a theme: by use or by type of wood for example. Popular storage boxes include cutlery boxes which range from open cutlery trays to upright knife boxes. Tea caddies are another popular

RIGHT *A witty collection of marquetry treen eggs and a string box sit on an Adam-style table with satinwood banding and inlay, decorated with painted medallions and garlands.*

item to collect; they can be found in other materials too, such as silver, porcelain and tin. Wooden tea caddies varied in style, some simple, others ornately inlaid with mother-of-pearl, ivory or other fine woods.

Sewing or writing boxes were also made in vast quantities. Today a few are still used for their original purpose but they make attractive and useful containers and are often more attractive than modern containers. Larger boxes can be placed on the floor, and medium-sized ones look good on bookshelves to break up a run of books.

CARE AND REPAIR

Small items should be dusted regularly with a soft cloth that will not catch on delicate veneers. Use wax sparingly and make sure it is well rubbed in — a greasy, sticky surface will attract dust. Use a good quality wax, not a spray, and build up the patina evenly and over time. This will also help to seal the wood. If the piece has metal locks, handles or other ornamentation, do not use metal polishes as they may eat into the wood or cause stains, just keep them waxed and polished. Repairs and stain removal should always be carried out by an expert.

In order to avoid the swelling and shrinkage that cause wood to warp and split, keep wooden items, furniture in particular, at constant temperature and levels of humidity. They will repay you well for the care.

RIGHT *A classic sideboard arrangement for a formal dining room. A silver samovar is flanked by a pair of matching knife boxes.*

BASKETS

Inexpensive and ubiquitous, baskets are a decorative accessory that everyone can use. Historically, baskets were used in everyday life to a far greater extent than they are today. Farmers used them to collect their crops, fishermen used them to store their catches and vendors used them at market to display their produce and make their deliveries. The styles and forms of the baskets depended on the plants that grew in the area, the use to which the basket was to be put and local traditions of decoration and design.

WOOD, FIBRES AND BARK

The material used will determine the natural colour of the basket and, to some extent, the intricacy of the weave. In England, the commonest material used in basketry is willow, which is strong and elegant but it does not have the elasticity of other materials and is therefore commonly used for large, straight-sided baskets, such as the log and dog baskets so frequently found in English country houses. Other traditional English baskets are the

ABOVE *A traditional English wicker picnic hamper with its original white china and fitted tin sandwich boxes. It is hard to find elegant sets like this as most of them have long since been split up.*

LEFT *Baskets were a very important household item to the early settlers in America. They made them out of local materials and used them to store just about everything. This is an early hand-painted and coloured split wood basket sitting on a Pennsylvania German painted chest.*

FAR LEFT *A lovely rustic jumble. The two baskets on the right are typical of the kind used for marketing in France and Italy. The other three are of English willow. Pale willow baskets are made from willow rods that have been peeled prior to soaking. (The rods have to be soaked to make them malleable). Darker baskets are made from rods that are soaked with their bark left on.*

Sussex trug, a curved open basket made from split wood commonly used as a garden basket, and the Somerset willybutt, a deep willow basket used by farmers for collecting fruit.

The traditional basketry of Native Americans reached a very high level of skill and intricacy of design, particularly in the Southwest. They made baskets for storage and carriage, they made sieves, threshing baskets, back packs, fish and bird traps, mats, cradles and even baskets for carrying water and for cooking. And they made them from a huge variety of materials, from rushes, grasses, roots and barks.

Baskets are common to practically every culture, and although today they are largely made for their decorative qualities and for the tourist trade, it does not make them any the less attractive when piled around the house.

USING AND DISPLAYING BASKETS

Basketwork plant holders make attractive accessories, although they will require a terracotta or plastic liner. They can be painted or decorated with ribbon trim to tie

ABOVE *This assorted collection of baskets hangs from the ceiling of this character-filled country kitchen on old butcher's hooks attached directly to the rafters.*

BELOW *A blue accent on a lovely old pine sideboard. An oval basket has been painted a striking shade of blue to match the planter with its profusion of grape hyacinths.*

in with your colour scheme. The same shape can double as a waste paper basket which, although not entirely practical, will serve well in bedrooms and can be cheaply replaced. Baskets have long been used for displaying and storing food. Fruit and vegetables look wonderful piled generously into baskets. Use them as table centrepieces or as substitutes for floral arrangements. In the sitting room, large baskets can store logs and magazines, small ones can hold potpourri or sweets. In bedrooms and bathrooms what better than a selection of baskets for soaps, cotton wool, make up and dirty laundry. For the hall you could find baskets of an appropriate shape to store boots, umbrellas and walking sticks. At table, a basket lined with a linen table napkin is both stylish and practical for bread, and for everyday use, basket-weave tablemats are extremely convenient, especially with children around.

I find the best way to store baskets when not in use is to hang them up. Most have handles in one form or another and they can hang in the kitchen with pots and pans on meat hooks, or from a hook in the wall, or on rods or poles. Baskets, for the most part cheap and cheerful, fill up dull spaces anywhere in the house and give the place some atmosphere.

ABOVE *This is part of my collection of baskets that hangs from a
curtain pole under a shelf in my kitchen. When I need to use one,
I just slip off the knob at the end. For the most part, though, I am
happy with them just as they are – as a decoration.*

NATURAL MATERIALS

Collectors and craftsmen have always been interested in the possibilities inherent in materials like shells, polished rocks, semi-precious stones and minerals, and products of the hunt such as ivory and bone. Ivory is, quite rightly, subject to many restrictions now, but old ivory is still to be found that does not encourage the continued slaughter of elephants. In any case, not all old ivory came from elephants, but from the fossilized remains of long-dead mammoths.

Tortoiseshell, which is quite easy to work, was often formed into beautiful combs or little trinket boxes edged and clasped with silver. It has been a popular material with collectors since the seventeenth century. Stones and shells became fashionable collectibles in the early nineteenth century when more and more intrepid travellers returned with trophies from their far-flung quests for knowledge of strange places and even stranger flora and fauna.

ABOVE *Victorian decorative shellwork plaques and boxes. Victorian ladies were constantly devising decorative schemes for their homes, often following patterns and ideas in books and magazines. Some of this work may well have been created by Victorian ladies as an amusing and instructive pastime.*

LEFT *A collection of meerschaum pipes and their associated boxes and holders. Meerschaum is a soft, easy to carve, mineral mined in Turkey. It was exported in large quantities to Vienna, Budapest and Paris in the 18th and 19th centuries, and became very popular for making pipes and cigarette holders. Many pipe bowls were carved into the shape of popular personalities and animals. Meerschaum is the German for sea-foam, as it was believed at the time to be petrified sea-foam.*

ABOVE *An extensive collection of tortoiseshell hair combs, carefully pinned with tacks onto a bedroom wall. Tortoiseshell was mainly taken from the shell of the small hawksbill sea turtle. The paler among these combs are made from horn. Both materials become malleable when heated, and can be cut, moulded and pressed into shape. The fashion for elaborate hair combs subsided with the advent of shingled hair in the 1920's.*

RIGHT *An unusual desk set decorated with silver, brass and semi-precious stones. The blue stones on the little envelope and writing paper chest and the blotter pad are of lapis lazuli and the green stone inset into the brass lid of the cut glass inkwell is a malachite.*

BOOKS FOR DISPLAY

There is no doubt that books furnish a room: they make it look lived-in, friendly and used. It is also undeniable that some books do it better than others. Dog-eared paperbacks are for reading, not for display, but leather-bound volumes and elegant hardbacks add a warm and witty feeling to the classic drawing room.

BOOKS ON SHELVES

Break up rows of books with ornaments — vases, small drawings or sculptures — or even with a small stack of books placed horizontally. You may find a few books in your collection with front covers far too beautiful to hide away, in which case display them face on and enjoy them, some covers are as exquisite as etchings.

Bookshelves need to be well lit, but not too brightly. If the shelves are made of glass, then one strip light concealed under the moulding at the top of the unit will be sufficient. Wooden shelves may need a light source for each shelf and the easiest way to do this is to use a flexible tube light running around the perimeter of the unit.

ABOVE *Part of a set of Cicero's works traditionally finished with hand-tooled leather bindings and bands of ornament gilding. The raised banding is known as 'blind' binding.*

BELOW *The purpose-built library shelves of a castle in Antwerp, Belgium. What can be seen of the walls is appropriately covered in tooled Spanish leather.*

ABOVE *Part of my bookshelves – the terracotta figures I sculpted myself.*

RIGHT *A bookish corner with old leather-bound books and paperweights.*

FAKES

If books are to be the theme of a room, and you do not have the contents of a library to hand, it is very easy to fake it. Leather-bound spines can be bought by the yard to conceal cupboard doors. There are door stops and paper weights, video covers, jewellery safes, book ends and box files disguised to look like erudite reading matter. There is even a wallpaper, convincingly designed to look like shelves of beautiful leather-bound books, that looks very effective indeed when used sparingly in alcoves and small hallways.

BOOK-RELATED FURNITURE

Antique lecterns, whether free-standing or table-top, look right in a bookish atmosphere. Their purpose is to make the reading of large-format reference books easier, and the bonus is that books can be left open on a particularly attractive spread for all to appreciate. Library steps are another bookish accessory which can lead a double life as a mini shelving system. Some kinds fold down to form a useful stool or side table.

Smaller book-related items which are attractive enough to display are ornamental bookends, antique bookmarks, paper knives and magnifying glasses.

CARE AND REPAIR

Real books should be regularly and gently dusted along the tops of the pages with a feather duster, otherwise the dust will eat into the pages. Hardback covers just need

ABOVE *The shelving runs all around the room and fake spines are glued to the door to complete the illusion. Only the discreet brass handle gives the secret away.*

the occasional dust, but leather covers benefit from buffing with a soft cloth and a proprietary leather dressing. Unless you are an experienced book-binder, it is always advisable to get antique books repaired or rebound by an experienced professional.

TOYS

RIGHT *A corner of a nursery with a collection of valuable antique toys too precious for a child to play with, but with an immense appeal for the collector. The rocking horse, who has somehow lost his lower jaw over the years, is on a trestle-type rocking base that was introduced in the 1880's. It has its original leather saddle and a mane of real horsehair, and it probably dates from the turn of the century. The charming porcelain dolls are prettily displayed in a well-sprung, early Victorian toy pram.*

BELOW *Groups of old and new toy soldiers confronting one another for eternity. Displayed here on a bookcase, they liven up the rows of books, adding personality and colour. It is often hard to tread the line between displaying a collection as if it were something from a glass case in a museum and spreading the items all over the place, making it so low-key you hardly notice it. This is a good compromise.*

It was during the Regency period in England (1811–1820) that the nursery became a standard room in larger houses and from that time on, during the Victorian and Edwardian eras, toys and games were produced in greater volumes. The nursery was not only a playroom but also a schoolroom, where a governess would supervise lessons. As children spent so much of their day there, furniture came to be made specifically for the nursery. It was robust, child-sized and often copied from larger, adult pieces. These charming little chairs, desks and tables can still be found today and, along with old-fashioned toys or games, can provide an instant dose of atmosphere and nostalgia that today's bright plastic playthings could never impart.

On the whole antique toys are delicate items with both monetary and sentimental worth, and they should not be used as playthings but as objects for display. The quality of these toys was superb, many being works of art in their own right, and therefore of great interest to collectors, so it is wise to look twice before you turn out your attic and send a box of potentially valuable toys to the local boot sale.

Even simple toys were well made and great importance was attached to the development of a child's mind. Toy designers and manufacturers way back then were concerned not only with the teaching of basic skills but with concepts such as helping children to turn their fantasies and fears into reality. Because these early toys had no pre-programmed actions built into them, children were forced to rely on their imaginations, and if we look back in history there are clear examples of how these simple toys helped shape future careers.

One of my ancestors, Sir Winston Churchill, stated that his army career was influenced by many a game with his lead toy soldiers. I myself loved to play with dolls' houses, constantly re-arranging the furniture and redecorating the walls, and I have friends who loved dolls' clothes who have ended up in the fashion business, so there must be something in the theory!

ROCKING HORSES

The design of the rocking horse probably evolved from the saddle horse used in the tack room to hold saddlery and no doubt used by children to imitate brothers and sisters old enough to ride. Early examples exist from the seventeenth century, but the height of their popularity was in Victorian times. Because they were such attractive toys, in many cases often works of art, rocking horses were not confined to the nursery but were welcomed in other rooms of the house.

Early rocking horses had boat-shaped rockers and bore little resemblance to a real horse. They consisted of a seat held between two flat pieces of wood with a head attached to the front. They were often left undecorated except for a mane and a tail.

Carved rocking horses with free-standing legs attached to bow-shaped rockers emerged at around the end of the seventeenth century and this concept continued to develop throughout the eighteenth century as horses became painted and more finely detailed. The classic finish was a dappled grey. Real horsehair was used for the mane and tail and the saddlery was made of leather, copied in detail from the real thing.

By the 1880's the style of rocker changed from the bow shape to a trestle rocker which created a smooth back and forth movement. This design, although not as attractive as the bow rocker, was certainly a safer bet for the boisterous child, it took up less space and was kinder to wall and floor surfaces as it tended not to travel.

Today there are quite a few rocking horse manufacturers who can copy these traditional designs with great skill, and restore antique ones with sensitivity. If buying

LEFT *Here is an example of a rocking horse being used as a decorative accessory in a hallway. It makes a lovely shape against the blue and white wood panelled walls, and looks as good as any sculpture could.*

ABOVE *An early rocking horse with bow-shaped rockers that probably dates from the mid-18th century. It has been extensively restored with brand new leather bridle and saddle, but it still has a simple naive charm.*

LEFT AND BELOW *A handmade town-house style of dolls' house with Georgian detailing to the exterior. The furnishing and the layout give some clues to the lifestyle of the period. Below stairs the kitchen staff sweep and clean and cook, and dry the clothes by passing them through an old-fashioned iron mangle with wooden rollers. In the drawing room-cum-dining room above, the sideboard is set with silver and glass. In the bedroom there is a washstand complete with ewer and bowl and a discreet chamber pot tucked away beneath. For an authentic touch, it is possible to buy, from specialist shops, books of doll's house wallpaper with reduced-scale patterns.*

an antique horse, look for original paintwork, a mane and tail of real horsehair, a well-shaped head with strong features picked out in paint and worn leather saddlery.

DOLLS' HOUSES

The earliest antique dolls' houses date from the first part of the eighteenth century. Many of them are such works of art that it fills me with horror to think of small children playing with them, but perhaps they were originally intended more for show than as toys, and I am sure that many an adult derived pleasure from them.

Much has been learnt from these dolls' houses about the way of life in grand houses of the period, down to the details of kitchen utensils used. This is not entirely surprising as many of the great architects and cabinet makers at one time or another became involved in the designing and furnishing of dolls' houses. Some replicas of well-known houses were made, such as Nostell Priory, designed by Robert Adam in 1733. This dolls' house, or

baby house as they were then called, is still completely intact with original furniture made by a young Thomas Chippendale who worked on the house as apprentice to the main carpenter.

Other less ornate houses may have been models made by architects to try and sell their ideas to prospective clients. The sale made, and the model being of no further use, it was often left with the family concerned, ending up in the nursery.

It was not only in England that dolls' houses were popular, but in Germany where the craze started even earlier, spreading soon to Holland where the Dutch went in for lavish interior details. The French, on the other hand, preferred individual room sets to houses. Later dolls' houses were more robust and larger in scale, more townhouse in style, and without the fine architectural details used in the past to impress admiring guests rather than sticky-fingered children. Much of the furniture for these more child-friendly houses originated from Germany.

BELOW *Appealing dolls with pretty porcelain faces. Early toy bears were first made in Germany. They had humped backs and long noses like the bears in this crib.*

ABOVE *An elegant double-fronted dolls' house with sophisticated period detail. Like rocking horses, good-looking early doll's houses can adorn rooms other than nurseries.*

Restoring old dolls' houses is an absorbing and time-consuming hobby. I have been attempting to restore one for about ten years and one day I hope to have the time to complete it. The difficulties are in finding architectural features and furniture in the correct scale to suit a particular style of house. The best places to look are toy fairs or auctions, although you may have to be patient to find all the items you need. Your efforts will be well rewarded though: as a decorative object a dolls' house will give endless pleasure.

DOLLS

Dolls have been made all over the world for many generations and out of just about any available material. Antique dolls complete with their original costumes look very attractive, but I find them difficult to display as ideally they should be kept behind glass, sealed away from dust and deterioration.

The most valuable are the bisque dolls, made from a type of unglazed porcelain. They were beautifully made and look incredibly lifelike which endears them to children. The best of these were produced in France and will have the maker's mark stamped on the body or the head.

Cheaper moulded copies were mass-produced in Germany and these will usually be marked with the mould number.

TIN TOYS

There is a great deal of interest among collectors in early tin toys such as toy soldiers, trains, cars, boats and planes. Many of the antique toy cars give a real insight into the cars that were being used at the time and the colours that were popular with early motorists. Tin toys are very appealing and now that age has mellowed their colours they make delightful displays that would not look at all out of place even in formal settings.

If you have inherited a lot of old toys with sentimental strings attached, it is hard to decide what to keep and display and what to leave in the attic, as some toys, such as old train sets, require a lot of space to be appreciated at their best. Sometimes it is better to sell and re-invest the money in another piece more suited to exhibition.

BELOW *Adjustable shelves in the corner of a sunny nursery make a natural showcase for a collection of tin trains and station buildings.*

ABOVE *An imaginative way to display a beautiful antique bisque doll. She has been perched in a period pram of enamelled tin.*

DECORATIVE FURNITURE

LARGE PIECES OF FURNITURE GIVE A ROOM ITS FORM AND DETERMINE HOW PEOPLE WILL GROUP TOGETHER AND HOW THEY WILL MOVE FROM ONE AREA OF A ROOM TO ANOTHER. BUT IT IS THE SMALL PIECES OF DECORATIVE FURNITURE THAT GIVE A ROOM ITS CHARACTER. FROM TABLE LAMPS TO SIDE TABLES, FROM PLANT STANDS TO SIDE CHAIRS, THESE NON-ESSENTIAL ITEMS MAKE A HOME THAT IS DISTINCTIVELY IDIOSYNCRATIC.

SMALL FURNITURE

Small pieces of antique furniture are an unbeatable way of adding character to a room with a visible link to the past. As an added bonus such pieces tend to hold their prices, if not increasing in value as time goes by.

Until the seventeenth century, furniture was fairly utilitarian. It became more decorative as craftsmen and architects travelled throughout Europe exchanging ideas and styles and publishing design books. Wealthy home-owners competed to commission the latest in fashionable pieces, often relating in style or design detail to the room in which they were to be displayed.

BELOW A japanned dressing table with a fold-down mirror adds a decorative touch to a bedroom. The finely-worked and gilded table is in the French taste and is flanked by a pair of chairs in the same style.

MIX AND MATCH

Unfortunately we cannot all afford to furnish our homes with precious antiques and, in some cases, say if you live in a very hot climate or near a beach, it may not even be practical. Another consideration is that the antiques you have acquired may not sit happily together. Some combinations, such as heavy Continental baroque and delicate English eighteenth-century would detract from one another, looking far better separated into different rooms and mixed with contemporary furniture.

In this section I want to mention alternative ways of furnishing your home without having to break the bank. With clever use of decorative pieces, perhaps mixed in with the odd good piece of antique furniture, it should be possible to achieve any number of effects. Reasonably-priced contemporary decorative pieces can include painted furniture, good quality reproductions and cane, wicker, bamboo and metal items.

ABOVE *An elegant gilt wood console table – the type of table designed to be displayed against a wall – is decorated with guilloche banding and festoons of flowers and leaves.*

BELOW *Behind the sofa in this elegant English sitting room, is a late 18th century satinwood occasional table with a top that folds out to make a circle.*

TABLES AND DESKS

Occasional tables serve many useful and decorative purposes. They are often used as what I call 'infillers': beside or behind a sofa or armchair, in an alcove or recess either side of a chimney breast or as a focal point at the end of a passage. They can have practical uses too, such as hall tables, games tables or coffee tables to hold trays or books.

SIDE TABLES

The most popular antique side tables are tripod tables with a tilting top which were originally designed for serving tea or supper (they are also referred to as tea or supper tables). Examples with pie-crust tops and ornate carving on the legs can command a high price, but simpler versions in mahogany or walnut are still affordable.

I often substitute a round table draped with a cloth for an antique table — however, the cost of one of these can sometimes be misleading. The base and top can be made of chipboard, but if an expensive fabric is used for the

BELOW *At Washington's house in Mount Vernon, Virginia, a classic Pembroke table is laid for tea, dominated by a silver samovar. The Chippendale style chairs are upholstered in a golden silk brocade to match the sofa.*

ABOVE *A heavy gilt side table looks good against a plain white wall. The ornamentation of wheat ears and bacchic masks suggests it may have been designed for a dining room.*

RIGHT *A black japanned tray on a new low base makes a successful coffee table. The circular table is of chipboard, made elegant with a full circular fringed brocade cloth.*

cover and trimmed with a deep fringe, the price will soon add up to that of a modest antique.

Another popular choice for a side table is a painted piece. They come in many standard designs, but a competent craftsman can make one to your own specifications. The paint finish can be whatever you want, from a simple country stipple, a wood grain or marble effect to a grand rich lacquer picked out in gilt.

I love old trays either made from painted *tôle* or *papier mâché* and they make attractive tables when placed on a base of *faux* bamboo or something equally light and leggy. If you are lucky enough to find a very large tray, it would make a wonderful coffee table.

COFFEE TABLES

These are the most difficult pieces of furniture in a house to get right. They did not exist in the past, therefore no

genuine antique ones exist. If you are trying to recreate a totally period room, say of classic Georgian style, then coffee tables are out, but these days living rooms need to be much more practical. One of the best solutions is to mix a bit of old with a bit of new: old screen or door panels under glass, fixed to a modern base, or an old tray as mentioned before. Antique fabrics or tapestries under glass make interesting tabletops too.

For a more modern approach, I often suggest the use of glass and perspex. This style will complement all other

ABOVE An unusual low table made from a old panel of marble with a carved border. The base of the table is made from two stone pediments.

types of furniture and works extremely well where space is limited as it gives the illusion of taking up no space. If you put a glass table over a beautiful patterned rug you get the added bonus of seeing more of the rug. Incidentally, glass-topped tables are also suitable for dining areas where space is limited for the same reason.

For a more contemporary feel, glass can be mixed with brass and other metals, although to me brass and glass is more suited to an office environment. Bases of wrought iron, perhaps with a verdigris finish, look good outdoors or in conservatories. They can be made up for you by a craftsman and teamed with tops of bevelled plate glass, stone or marble.

DESKS AND WRITING TABLES

Most antique desks were designed for their aesthetics, beautiful *objets* made for the pleasure of the letter writer, amateur poet or diarist and not at all suitable for today's computers, fax machines and telephones. The earliest type of writing table was the knee hole desk, which was more like a small chest with one long drawer along the top, small drawers down each side and a slightly recessed cupboard in the centre. They were mostly made in

BELOW *A large, low glass table with the thinnest of iron frames brings a sparkle to a sunny room. A glass coffee table allows you to enjoy the illusion of space.*

ABOVE *A papier mâché* tray on a base of faux *bamboo that has been painted and gilded to match. The combination makes a convincing and practical coffee table.*

figured woods such as walnut. Knee hole desks are really too small to serve as working desks and consequently are more often consigned to the bedroom where they make very pretty dressing tables.

Other popular small desks are known in Britain as davenports. They were first made around the beginning of the nineteenth century. They have a sloping leather inset top, often with a brass gallery, placed above a set of side-opening drawers. These and other ladies' small writing desks make wonderful infillers in all rooms, but are rarely used now for their original purpose.

Pedestal desks, partners' desks and library tables were introduced in the mid-eighteenth century and continue to be the most popular and practical form of desk, well suited to the home office or study especially when teamed up with a leather chair to match their leather tops. The style of these working desks has changed very little — their legs are perhaps the best guide to deciphering their age. The earliest examples have square, tapering legs and plain tops, leading on to delicate turned legs,

sometimes with reeding. Victorian writing tables are much heavier in style with wide, turned legs more in keeping with their confident, gothic styles of architecture and interior design.

BUREAUX AND SECRETAIRES

For rooms that need a piece of beautiful furniture with substance, both bureaux and secretaires would be appropriate. They are extremely elegant pieces that need to be placed against a wall, so making good focal points as well as being of real practical use.

Most bureaux have a hinged flap which folds down to form a flat writing surface supported by two pull-out arms, and a chest of drawers beneath. Bureau bookcases follow the same form but combine a cabinet or bookcase above. These make very attractive living room pieces, with the top housing books or a collection of porcelain and the hinged base either left open or closed.

Secretaires vary from bureaux in the form of the writing surface, which in the secretaire is a top false drawer that opens and slides out.

In the case of both secretaire bookcases and bureau bookcases, it is important to ensure that the top and base

ABOVE *A late 18th century desk with particularly attractive brass handles. It is important never to change the handles on a piece as it will reduce its value. You can tell if the handles are original by looking inside the drawer and checking for redundant screw holes or other give-away signs. Handles tend to mean 18th century, knobs the 19th.*

LEFT *A detail of the interior of a typical 18th century bureau cabinet. The top has pull-out candlestands, and behind the cupboard doors above the desk are more cupboards and compartments. Sometimes these pieces were spoiled by having the doors replaced with glass to show off the intricate carpentry.*

ABOVE *A lovely glass-fronted bookcase makes a natural focal point in any room.*

are both original and not 'marriages' as this will lower their value considerably.

It is possible to find very good quality reproduction desks in all shapes and styles which are certainly more affordable than the real thing and probably more functional. Painted desks are neither particularly attractive nor practical, except for children's rooms, and I would not advocate using them in a room where they will be subject to scrutiny.

CHAIRS AND STOOLS

There are many chairs I would place firmly in the decorative category of chairs that were never designed to be sat on at all. Understandably such chairs are more suited to hallways and bedrooms where they can be admired but not used a great deal.

Traditional hall chairs have upright backs and hard seats. Their intended position was up against the wall and their purpose was to impress rather than to offer rest and comfort. Indeed the backs were often decorated with carvings of such an elaborate nature that leaning back in them would be virtually impossible.

Decorative chairs were often made for specific areas, like corner chairs, first made in the early Georgian period, which were built diagonally with a double-sided back. The curio chair is another impractical yet highly decorative item. In this category come chairs decorated with shells or made entirely of antlers or with every part decoratively twisted and turned.

ABOVE *A typical pair of hall chairs with armorial crests. These are painted on, but crests were often elaborately carved. Such chairs were usually made of solid, very grand woods such as mahogany. Hall chairs are often found in sets since they were placed around the hall for visitors to wait on. When they were not being sat upon, the decorative backs made an impact against the walls.*

LEFT *A pair of pretty painted decorative chairs placed either side of a fireplace for balance.*

ABOVE *An American curio chair that has been created from quaintly-shaped branches and twigs.*

BELOW *This is quite a comfortable decorative chair by William Morris and Co., from the English Arts and Crafts era. It is a typical pure and simple design, made of ebonized wood with a rush seat.*

More aesthetically pleasing are lacquered and japanned chairs from the early eighteenth century, which are fine and delicate, especially those with cane seats. They should be used as decorative pieces in bedrooms or either side of a piece of furniture for balance.

Throughout the Regency period in England, furniture became more decorative and less traditional. Influenced by classical French and Italian designs, the chairs of this period incorporated motifs such as animal heads and feet. Comfort was low on the list of priorities. Chairs produced around the turn of the century were no better in the comfort stakes. These styles were influenced and often made by the great designers of the time such as the Scottish architect and designer Charles Rennie Mackintosh. They were used to make a style statement rather than provide a practical form of seating, and that is how they should be used today.

DINING CHAIRS

Most early dining chairs were made in sets of fourteen, comprising twelve singles and two carvers. Today you frequently find the sets split in half and sold as one set of six singles and another set of eight including the carvers. It is very difficult to find original complete sets of dining chairs and if you do, the price will be prohibitive. Most people will be content to buy a set of six or eight and if they need any more, have them copied by an expert craftsman — for amateurs it will be difficult to distinguish between old and new.

I frequently recommend people to mix sets of chairs, either buying several matching pairs in similar styles or by having complete contrasts. For example, if you have a good set of period originals, get another set of upholstered high-back chairs and alternate them around the table, it can look very attractive.

Reproduction high back upholstered chairs are a very

ABOVE A set of modern, high back dining chairs upholstered in a classic stripe with blue moiré backs. They make a comfortable and stylish setting, the fabric picking up the yellows, reds and blues used elsewhere in the room.

RIGHT There is a full set of dining chairs here, but there is no way of telling which are reproductions and which are the real thing. The original upholstery is preserved (or hidden) from view with a smart set of white summer covers to match the lace table linen, the white floor tiles and the pale stone walls.

reasonable alternative to period chairs. The legs can often be made to suit the style of the rest of your furniture at little extra cost and they can be upholstered in a variety of ways, including slip covers with skirts that cover the backs or the legs or both. The advantage of slip covers is that they can be whisked off and changed to create different looks for different occasions.

Dining chairs need to be comfortable, which generally means either upholstered seats or cushions. Cushions, apart from the comfort they bring, can introduce an

ABOVE *A very elegant set of pale, painted wooden chairs, complete with carver, discreetly upholstered in a steely-blue fabric that picks up the blue from the stripes on the chairs.*

accent of colour into your dining area. Depending on the style of your room, the cushions can be trimmed with contrasting piping or rope and secured to the chair with simple ties, elaborate rope and tassels or more feminine bows. It is always wise to have zippered covers so they can be taken off and cleaned.

LEFT *A set of Victorian side chairs flanking a marble-topped chest of drawers. Chairs such as these were mass-produced in infinite numbers and in thousands of different patterns to display elaborate bobbin turning techniques that had just become feasible thanks to the advent of new machinery.*

BELOW *Late 18th century French chairs, of a typically restrained and elegant design, beautifully upholstered with antique tapestry panels. The tapestry is disintegrating a little on the left hand chair, but I think it is better to keep it like that and enjoy looking at them rather than recovering with a modern fabric.*

CLASSIC CHAIRS

Many of today's reproduction chairs are copied from the designs of great eighteenth century English cabinet makers such as Thomas Chippendale and George Hepplewhite, and chairs made to their designs are referred to by their names. These elegant pieces give an instant classic accent to any scheme. Other popular designs originated from France, such as the Louis XV and Louis XVI *fauteuils* and *bergères*. The way in which they are finished can determine their degree of grandeur: a gilt finish with upholstery of silk damask would be more suited to a grand drawing room, but the same chair with a limed oak or painted finish and a contemporary fabric could be used in most settings.

EASY CHAIRS

Comfortable seats with upholstered arms, seats and backs were developed in the late seventeenth century. One of the earliest types was the Queen Anne style wing chair with high sides and wings to shield the occupant

RIGHT *A large Victorian buttoned stool, upholstered in wool damask with a deep wool fringe, acts here as a coffee table. On top, a tôle tray provides the necessary rigid surface for putting down glasses and cups.*

BELOW *A wing chair in the design associated with the late 17th, early 18th century, and much reproduced. It is both comfortable and elegant. This one has stretchers, but many examples have fine cabriole legs.*

from draughts and the heat of the open fire. Wing chairs and library chairs are still popular fireside chairs in sitting rooms and look their best upholstered in heavy-weight fabrics such as velvets, damasks and chenilles.

In the Victorian era, easy chairs became increasingly popular as the demand for comfort superseded elegance. The popular button-back chair was developed at this time along with the tub chair and the nursing chair, all of which are frequently copied today. It is from these beginnings that today's ubiquitous, fully-upholstered armchair finally evolved.

STOOLS

Stools make wonderful occasional and decorative pieces of furniture and, in my view, are often under used. Simple, three-legged stools have been around for hundreds of years. Joint stools, which have four turned legs held together by an apron, date from the middle of the sixteenth century. They had flat wooden seats, sometimes with a loose cushion on top, but were never upholstered.

These straightforward stools were usually made of oak or elm.

Upholstered stools became popular in the late eighteenth century. Less robust woods, such as walnut, were used in order to match the stools to other elegant pieces of drawing room furniture, and the shape of the legs changed from the simple turned or square to cabriole, delicately carved with ball and claw feet. Tops were upholstered to match chairs and, by the Victorian era,

ABOVE *19th century chairs covered in scraps of old kilim rugs are perfectly suited to this rich, red room with its hand-painted walls and ceiling.*

the tops were being deep buttoned to match their chesterfields and arm-chairs. The Victorians also made footstools and ottomans which they enjoyed enriching with elaborate upholstery and by adding embellishments, such as gilding, to the wood.

Most types of stool can be bought as reproductions these days, and they are relatively inexpensive. They can look extremely effective and decorative, especially if they are upholstered in an imaginative way — perhaps with kilim rugs or some other showcase piece of fabric. Stools are not always square or rectangular. Look for round ones, ovals, trefoils or ones with interestingly-shaped corners: these are more of a challenge to upholster but they add a real touch of interest to a room.

The practical aspect of the stool should not be forgotten. Apart from supplying additional seating space, box ottomans with hinged lids provide extra storage space, and large stools with flat tops, or even firmly upholstered ones, make excellent substitutes for coffee tables.

ABOVE *A box ottoman used as a coffee table. It is covered in a suitably oriental material – old carpeting. The form of the ottoman derived from a low, broad Turkish upholstered bench which became hugely popular in the 19th century, particularly for Turkish-style rooms, like this one. The Turkish style was a favourite for men's smoking rooms.*

RIGHT *In complete contrast to the warm richness of the room above, the spare, clean lines of this supremely elegant x-frame stool of Regency or Empire origin, set the tone for this classic, uncluttered room.*

RACKS AND STANDS

Hat and coat stands first appeared in the nineteenth century and were made in both wood and cast iron. Antique versions are more satisfactory than modern replicas as they are much heavier and do not topple over so easily. They require quite a bit of space, and therefore are not practical for small town houses with narrow entrance halls. A more suitable alternative in this case would be hooks, either fixed directly onto the wall or mounted onto a piece of wood. Where possible, use old brass hooks and a mature piece of wood to give the coat rack a bit of character.

HAT STANDS

On its own, a hat stand can be used for a whole range of purposes. I have used them in kitchens to hang baskets, intermingled with strings of onions and garlic. I have seen them used in outer halls or downstairs cloakrooms to hold a combination of Wellington boots, gloves and

ABOVE A faux *bamboo plant stand used as an infill in the corner of an elegant bedroom. This was probably originally made as a candle stand or* torchère *and used for holding a candlestick or a candelabra, as it is a good height to cast light down on a table. The turned wood candlestand in the foreground is still being used for its original purpose.*

LEFT A *characterful country hallway with wall-fixed hooks and a new pine shelf above.*

BELOW *A Victorian cast iron umbrella stand looks quite at home in this leafy conservatory. The stand is in the gothic revival style.*

RIGHT *An astonishing ironwork stick and umbrella stand that was never intended to be concealed in a subtle corner. But for all its ostentation it is also practical – it has detachable pans at the base for catching the drips from wet umbrellas.*

ABOVE *A collection of walking sticks, fencing foils and a candle-snuffer are gathered in a timeless terracotta crock.*

scarves. In conservatories or garden rooms, painted cast iron hat stands can look very attractive holding hanging baskets of flowers and plants.

CANDLE AND LAMP STANDS

Guèridons and *torchères* are portable (but only just) stands that were originally moved from room to room and used to support candlesticks or lamps. Their designs were varied, more often than not hugely ornate, and they were made in pairs with a table and mirror to match. Today they are more widely used as plant stands as few of us have the need for candlesticks in each room, or indeed possess candlesticks large enough to sit upon them without looking ridiculous.

UMBRELLA STANDS

These are really useful and decorative pieces of hall furniture that do not particularly lend themselves to any other uses other than the intended. They can be found in a variety of materials including iron, wood, bamboo,

RIGHT *An unusual triangular set of wooden shelves, probably made to house a particular collection of objects. Now it is a display case for a set of* trompe l'oeil *ceramic jugs, painted to look like wood. The urn-shaped cache-pot in the foreground is of treen, or turned hardwood.*

BELOW *A pretty metal hanging shelf with a distinctly Regency feel.*

brass and porcelain, and obviously the style you choose will depend on where it is to be placed. Personally, I favour wood or brass. Modern porcelain stands, generally made in the Far East or Portugal, can suit town houses or apartments if they are chosen in a colour to tie in with the overall scheme.

DECORATIVE STANDS AND SHELVES

Other interesting and decorative stands include antique music stands, which can help fill a bare corner in a room, perhaps displaying a book instead of sheet music. Old shaving stands, which incorporate a tilting mirror and a small table, sometimes with a hinged lid for storage, can make attractive and useful pieces for bathrooms and cloakrooms. Hanging shelves became popular in the late eighteenth century – before that most shelves were built in or incorporated into bookcases or dressers. Original designs were simple, made mostly of mahogany and Chinese or gothic in style with fretwork or solid ends. They were usually quite small, sometimes incorporating cupboards, in which case they make ideal bathroom cabinets; sometimes with delicate little shelves that make them perfect for displaying small collections. Small hanging shelves make lovely decorative pieces for any room and can be painted to tie in with a particular colour scheme or left in their natural wood.

TABLE LAMPS

Lamps make wonderful decorative pieces, while adding plenty of atmosphere to a room. The light they give is softer than overhead lighting and, if you use them with shades of different colours, you can vary the look to suit your scheme and the desired level of light.

The earliest purpose-built electric lamps date from the late nineteenth century, and the large number of lamps that were produced at that time have now become collectors' items. Particularly decorative and popular were those made in the *Art Nouveau* style by Tiffany, Lalique and Gallé. The real things are very expensive, but convincing contemporary copies can be found at much less than the original cost.

ANTIQUE LAMPS

There is no such thing, of course, as an antique electric lamp. What we refer to as antique lamps are generally antique vases, gas or oil lamps or candelabra that have been converted and electrified. Antique vases from the Far East and from the famous porcelain factories of Europe can be easily converted into lamps by adding a simple turned wooden base (this means you do not have to drill into the porcelain and so reduce its value) and a brass top plate to hold the lamp holder. Obviously it is not an intelligent move to convert a valuable antique vase as it will lose its value and could be damaged.

SHADES

Personally, I think antique-style lamps look best teamed with traditional silk shades, although in a more contemporary setting lacquered card could be suitable. The shape of the shade will depend on the scale and shape of the lamp. It is always wise to take the lamp with you when buying a shade so you can make sure that the

ABOVE *An Art Nouveau inspired lamp with an opaque glass shade reminiscent of an oil lamp. It gives just the right kind of period glow to the dark green walls, the rich oil paintings and the handsome brass-faced clock.*

LEFT *A mixture of table lamps, sidelights and firelight suffuse this delightful room with interesting pools of light rather than a harsh overall sameness.*

LEFT *An early (in electrical terms) brass desk lamp with a flexible stem. It is being used to spotlight a serious marble bust and a collection of attractive oil paintings.*

BELOW *A lamp made from an oriental bronze vase, perfectly balanced with a plain white card shade. The relationship between the two is just right.*

proportions look good together. A further consideration when buying a shade is the position of the lamp and the amount of space the shade will occupy.

Cream silk provides a good, warm light. It can be used flat, gathered or pleated onto the shade frame and looks good finished with braid or fan-edging frills. Dark coloured silk absorbs light, so do not use it to make shades for working lights, but use dark silk shades to create a wonderful atmospheric glow.

Candelabra look best with individual shades on each bulb, as naked bulbs can give off a harsh light, especially at eye level. These individual shades generally clip straight onto the bulb and they need to be made of a heat-resistant material.

Oil and gas lamps would originally have had some type of glass shade. If converting an antique, try and find an old glass shade or a new one in a traditional shape.

MODERN LAMP BASES

Tall column shapes are useful where there is not much space, bulbous urn shapes are pretty but they do take up a lot of room on a table. Ceramic bases, both plain and

ABOVE *A pair of gilt wood candlesticks converted into table lamps. The dark card shades do not throw out much light.*

lamps, lanterns and wall lights, but it varies enormously in quality, finish and price. Solid brass is the most desirable but the most expensive. A tarnished brass finish always looks better than a bright lacquer, especially for traditional designs like column-shaped lamp bases. Brass is suitable for desk lights and floor-standing lamps as the weight of the brass will help them remain stable. Many brass lamps have brass shades which provide a more contemporary feel; they are good for reading and for working as they can be angled in any direction.

Traditional wooden standard lamps are useful, but they can look a little old-fashioned. A practical and attractive alternative would be a lamp table, which incorporates a standard lamp and a useful little table, commonly made in a combination of polished wood or painted lacquer and brass.

patterned, suit many situations and are available in an increasing variety of shapes. Wood is another popular material for lamp bases and modern machinery means they can be elaborately turned and shaped without costing a fortune. Finishes vary from natural polished hardwood to a variety of painted finishes to tie with virtually any decorative scheme.

Brass suits both modern and traditional styles of

UNUSUAL LAMP BASES

There is a trend at the moment for lamps made of *tôle* and large tea caddies copied from old designs but with a contemporary decorative finish. The most common colours used are Chinese lacquer red, green and black. They look good in both classical and contemporary settings. Clear, coloured and opaque glass is also used in lamp making. Combined with brass or silver it can be very attractive and, when lit, it gives a lovely sparkle.

RIGHT *Traditional column-shaped lamp bases in softly-glowing polished brass topped with classic shades.*

BELOW *A large tôle tea caddy makes a striking lamp base. The lovely old rose colour of the painted tin tones beautifully with the sponged green walls.*

OTHER DECORATIVE PIECES

RIGHT A baby grand in a music room that is obviously much in use. The three elegant antique music stands are lovely pieces in their own right. The lyre form is a classical reference to the lyre-playing Apollo, god of music and song.

Pianos and other keyboard instruments can have lives as decorative pieces of furniture even if they are never used for their original purposes. A baby grand piano can look extremely elegant and it provides an excellent surface over which you could drape an antique shawl and place a display of pretty objects. However, you would need a fair-sized room to show off a full grand to its best advantage.

FAR RIGHT A highly polished grand piano stands like a sculptural form in this imposing black and white tiled hall. It serves also as a useful surface for a really impressive flower arrangement.

Other keyboard instruments such as harpsichords can be very beautifully constructed with intricate inlay or delicate painting, and even if they are not playable, they make lovely pieces to look at.

Another decorative piece of furniture that can help fill an empty corner is a globe on a stand. These are also surprisingly useful and, rather like barometers, you will probably refer to them more a great deal often than you would think.

RIGHT On the elegant Regency sofa lies an inlaid classical guitar and on the right there stands a classic gilded and painted harp. Harps were very popular home musical instruments at the turn of the 19th century.

FIREPLACES AND ACCESSORIES

To me, a sitting room without a fireplace feels as though it is lacking something. Not only does a fire provide welcome additional heat in winter, it exudes a wonderful, welcoming ambience that positively invites people to come in, relax and sit down and instantly makes them feel at home.

If you are planning on replacing a fireplace or installing one, then it is important to choose, from among the numerous styles, one which is sympathetic to the architecture and the style of your interior. It is not essential to choose a period piece, but be wary, because the wrong size and style can ruin the overall effect of a room in a radical way.

Up until the eighteenth century, fireplaces were quite simply holes in the chimney breast with plain surrounds. In the eighteenth century, as houses became more lavish and decorative features became as important, if not more so, than practical ones, fireplaces became more and more sophisticated.

The style of the fire surround reflected the size and style of house. Modest homes had simple wood or stone surrounds while grand rooms boasted ornately carved

ABOVE *A late 18th century style firebasket designed for burning coal rather than large logs. The basket contains the fire and lifts it off the floor.*

BELOW *A large, early fireplace with a cast iron fireback to protect bricks and reflect heat. In the 17th century these were decorated with mythical scenes or heraldic ornamentations.*

marble. The designs used often reflected the ornamentation used in the rooms' ceiling mouldings and cornicing. In very grand houses, architects would design a different theme for such details in every major room.

Eighteenth-century fireplaces could afford to be more compact, as coal was replacing wood. The insides of the fireplaces changed too, to accommodate the use of coal, and small grates or fire baskets were used instead of large fire dogs or andirons supporting iron rods.

The first built-in grates appeared early in the eighteenth century as the free-standing grates that had been used to burn wood were too large and too dangerously close to the hearth. The fire basket was integrated into the hob grate and took up the whole width of the fireplace. It was at this time that fenders were introduced, used in front of the hearth to stop ashes or coals falling out of the newly-raised grates.

FIRE IRONS

Fireside tools were made in sets: pokers, tongs, brushes and small shovels with matching upright stands. Today we more commonly abandon the stand and use decorative firedogs or andirons to rest them on.

Fireside accessories in grander homes were made of brass or polished steel, while more modest households favoured cast iron. Whichever material you choose, it is better to stick to one rather than a mix of styles, although

some fire baskets do incorporate both steel and brass in the design which would give a carefully chosen mixture of fire irons some credence.

FIREBACKS AND FIRE SCREENS

Cast iron firebacks were originally used to protect the brickwork behind the fire. They were free-standing and decorated in a variety of ways, often incorporating a family's coat of arms or initials or some decorative detail reprised from the room. Today, firebacks are used more to decorate the back of the opening and can be incorporated into the side cheeks. If you cannot find a suitable old one, there are many talented craftsmen who will make them up to your design.

Fire screens, not to be confused with fire guards which are used to stop sparks from spitting out into the room, were originally used to protect a lady's complexion from the heat of the fire. Pole screens, with an adjustable panel, have been in existence for a long time, and can still be found, sometimes in pairs, and often incorporating panels of tapestry. They make lovely decorative items. Other upright screens, such as cheval screens, were made to sit in front of the fireplace and they can be put to practical use, hiding an empty opening or an unused fireplace during the summer months. There are plenty of modern screens that will also serve this purpose. They are usually made of tin and cut to look like a vase of flowers with a painted or découpage finish.

ABOVE A Victorian duck's nest grate in an unusually quirky fireplace. The mantelpiece is made from half a lamp stand base, a cornice moulding and a large amount of plaster of Paris. The fire irons are brass and the traditional coal scuttle is copper.

RIGHT This is a club fender, with a padded and upholstered top so people can perch next to the fire. Obviously any fabric this near a fire should be treated with fire-retardant. Victorians often used plain wood or leather, which is, of course, much safer.

ABOVE A pole screen with a height-adjustable panel for preserving ladies' delicate complexions from the heat of the fire.

DOOR FURNITURE

Until the early eighteenth century, door furniture was simple, utilitarian and made of wrought iron. The earliest hinges were pin hinges, where a pin is fixed to the door post, and a long metal strap to the door which drops down onto the pin and pivots as the door is opened and closed. In the elegant eighteenth century, hinges were concealed and made of brass. Latches and bolts were the order of the day before knobs and handles were introduced, and you can still find these in use today on some cottage and stable doors. The first type of brass rim locks were used in the late seventeenth century. In these, the door knob and lock were set into a metal box

LEFT *An 18th century panelled door with a fanlight above. The brass fittings of knocker, door knob and handle are probably original while the letter box and bell on the door jamb, are 19th century additions.*

ABOVE *A simple American Shaker door latch, wrought in iron, is an elegant design that works perfectly.*

RIGHT *Interior door furniture consisting of finger plates, handles and lock. The finger plate is inlaid with a mother-of-pearl family crest.*

ABOVE *Three original 18th century door knockers with different designs of female heads: the one on the far right is a rather unwelcoming gorgon.*

and mounted onto the door. Early versions had pull latches and later ones ran to handles and knobs. As the whole purpose of locks and hinges is to work efficiently, if you do buy old ones, make sure they have been thoroughly re-conditioned.

KNOBS AND KNOCKERS

Door knobs and handles became more decorative in the late eighteenth century when, along with other decorative

accessories, they were designed to complement the design of the room as a whole. Escutcheons appeared on locks, and finger plates appeared on doors, adding extra decoration as well as protecting polished wooden doors from marks and damage.

Door knockers, in a whole variety of shapes and sizes, were introduced in the early eighteenth century, but letter boxes and door bells were a much later addition. Today door furniture is available in hundreds of styles and finishes. The most popular finish is still brass, although most of it is plated and not solid. Ornate brass door furniture can be very expensive, so I would advise keeping to simple yet elegant styles for general use. If you need to match up an existing piece or require something specially made up, there are a few excellent foundries that can make to order.

Chrome fittings can be used to effect in kitchens and bathrooms to tie in with taps — in some cases I have used nickel-plated door knobs to match bathroom fittings. Plain or cut glass door knobs with brass or chrome plates can look very attractive, especially on bedroom doors, and porcelain knobs and finger plates look good, especially on unpainted wooden doors.

DOOR STOPS

You can make these decorative and highly practical items out of just about anything – a brick covered in tapestry or felt, or a polished stone. In hallways, purpose-made upright wrought iron or brass door stops are most popular but there is no reason why you could not use a bronze figure, carved wooden animals or those smooth lumps of glass known as 'dumps' made from the left-over bits of molten glass.

✳✳

FABRICS

FABRICS CLOTHE ROOMS WITH COLOUR AND TEXTURE AND FIX THE
ROOM'S PERSONALITY AND STYLE. SOME FABRICS, LIKE OLD
TAPESTRIES AND FIGURED DAMASKS, CAN BRING A TOUCH OF
BYGONE ELEGANCE TO ANY SETTING; OTHERS, LIKE HEAVY
VICTORIAN BROCADES, ARE FIRMLY FIXED IN THEIR ERA. PLAIN
LINENS AND FRESH FLORAL PRINTS CAN BE DRESSED UP IN ALL KINDS
OF WAYS, AND PLAIN WHITE COTTONS AND LACE ARE
ABSOLUTELY TIMELESS.

✳✳

WALL HANGINGS

Antique tapestries were often custom-made for grand houses and woven in silk or wool to designs appropriate to the owners. Some of the tapestries at my ancestral home, Blenheim, for example, depict Marlborough at the Battle of Blenheim. For this victory over the French, John Churchill, first Duke of Marlborough, was given the land and the wherewithal to build a suitably triumphant monument and palace by a grateful Queen Anne.

Valuable tapestries are often known by the name of the factory that made them, such as the famous French factory Gobelins. The detail achieved by many of these fine weavers is quite superb; the richness of the silk and the subtle use of colour adds real depth to the scenes.

Unfortunately, antique tapestries are beyond most budgets, but reproductions are made in a variety of sizes. Tapestries are particularly effective on large walls in an area where you can stand back and see them from a distance. They should be fixed either directly to the wall or hung from a pole and weighted at the base to help them hang straight.

LEFT *A white silk Spanish shawl has been fixed to the wall above this window, making an unusual pelmet that frames the window seat.*

BELOW *An embroidered Indian wall hanging is fixed to this white-painted stone wall on a hidden batten. Wall hangings often work better than pictures on rough-hewn walls.*

ABOVE *A beautiful 17th century Flemish tapestry with a characteristic design of lush vegetation and birds. The wide, more stylized border is another typical feature of tapestries of this period and provenance. The tapestry has been cleverly accessorized with bouquets of fruit and vegetables.*

For a more contemporary feel, painted wall hangings are probably more suitable. These are usually painted by a mural artist onto canvas and hung in the same way as tapestries. The subject matter can range from *trompe-l'oeil* sylvan scenes to abstract patterns.

QUILTS, RUGS, SHAWLS AND OTHER FABRICS

For those of us who do not possess antique tapestries or painted murals nor, indeed, walls large enough on which to hang them, there are plenty of alternatives.

Really any decorative, attractive piece of fabric – embroidery, tapestry, old curtains or rugs – can be hung on the wall. Either stretch the fabric onto a frame, loosely drape it over a pole, or hang it between a couple of

hooks or rings. If the fabric has an all-over design, it can be gathered or draped, but a more artistic subject should be kept flat so you can appreciate it as it was intended to be seen. If the edges are a bit tatty they can be trimmed and edged with a plain piece of suitable fabric or braid.

Antique patchworks and quilts make attractive wall hangings, especially the traditional American quilts that are works of art in their own right.

LEFT *Folkloric flat-weave rugs and throws featuring bees and bugs dominate this idiosyncratic bedroom. The Indian feel is reinforced by a painted wall hanging of horsemen, the richly embroidered cushions and the embroidered crewelwork bedspreads, one of which has been used as a curtain.*

BELOW *An Islamic-inspired wall hanging runs the length of the wall. It is attached to the wall by curtain rings sewn along the top edge.*

ABOVE *In an ancient stone-flagged Scottish house, a damask-patterned wall hanging and a length of crewelwork fabric hang from the walls.*

Beautiful rugs can be turned into wall hangings too. Old and fragile rugs that would no longer be practical on the floor can still be enjoyed and admired as wall hangings without inflicting any more wear and tear on them.

Antique shawls are another attractive idea for wall hangings. It is well worth picking up shawls and hangings on your travels, especially if you get to faraway places like India, Africa and the Far East, where the markets are full of bargain delights.

Wall hangings probably look best hung on plain walls rather than on patterned wallpaper which may detract or clash with the colours and designs. You can also intermingle wall hangings with paintings and other decorative objects on a wall, although if you do this, they should form part of a theme or style in which all the pieces relate to one another.

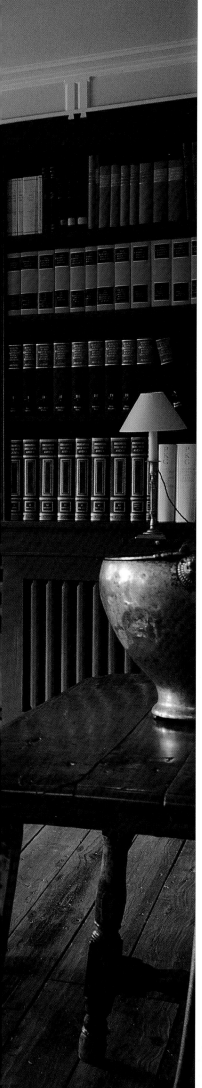

RUGS

Used on their own on a stone or wooden floor, or on top of a fitted carpet, rugs are one of the richest of decorative accessories. Antique rugs, and many contemporary ones for that matter, are a true art form, adding plenty of style, ambience and warmth to a room. Rugs have been made for hundreds of years in every corner of the world and their varied styles, designs and weaving techniques are all clues to their provenance.

ORIENTAL RUGS

The oldest and most influential country for fine carpet weaving was Persia (now Iran), but today, antique Persian rugs are very expensive and difficult to find intact. Sought-after rugs include those from Esfahan, produced in the seventeenth century, which have a wool pile and a silk and cotton base. Other popular later Persian pile carpets come from Heriz; they are rich in design and, like all good rugs, hardwearing. In the end, the value of an antique Persian rug comes down to its age, its condition, the rarity of the designs and colours, the number of knots per square inch, the state of the backing and the depth of the pile.

Fine quality and varied designs are the hallmark of Turkish rugs. They have produced magnificent flat

LEFT *The classic appeal of an antique oriental rug lies in the soft colours achieved by age and by the vegetable dyes used to colour the wools and silks before weaving. If you are putting a rug under a table or desk, it is advisable to shift it around so that it wears evenly.*

BELOW *The idea of using rugs as table overcloths came from Dutch 16th and 17th century interiors. It is an ideal way to use and enjoy a small fragile rug. The high-back caned and carved chairs are also reminiscent of the period.*

LEFT *A profusion of lovely colours are echoed and re-echoed in the portrait, the overcloth and the rug. The simple white curtains and blinds allow these colours to take centre stage. The colours in the rug are European in feel, while the design has a definite oriental leaning.*

RIGHT *A modern flat-weave kilim. This weaving technique does not produce the thickness and bulk of a pile carpet, so attractive specimens can be preserved by using them as throws. They are woven like tapestries, so they are reversible. They can be turned over during the sunny summer months to prevent the vegetable dyes from fading.*

weave kilims and piled rugs for many, many years. Kilims are popular and versatile and, while there are many antique examples – in particular the rare and beautiful 'Ushaks' from the west of Turkey – there are also a wonderful array of contemporary designs.

Modern kilims are both easy to come by and affordable. They look good in most settings, in particular on top of sisal matting or sea grass. In halls they provide a welcoming feel and a kilim runner in a narrow entrance not only makes the passage feel shorter and wider, it also provides practical protection to a fitted carpet or wood floor in a notoriously busy place. Other popular Turkish rugs are those from the Caucasus area which were made mostly between 1870 and 1920. They are thick-piled, rich in colour and not surprisingly popular with collectors.

EUROPEAN RUGS

Whilst rugs were being made by just about every local tribesman throughout Asia, rug-making was also prolific in Europe and in particular in France, where the designs

and techniques were influenced by Turkish styles.

The two main carpet workshops were those of Savonnerie and Aubusson. The Savonnerie factory made carpets from about 1627 to 1825 using oriental techniques and large classical motifs in the design. Their rugs were immensely popular, resulting in many other factories adopting their style and subsequently their name. Aubusson rugs were more like tapestries, woven with contemporary scenes of the eighteenth century. They are especially sought-after today as their subtle soft, faded colours make them easy to use in any room, adding an instant feel of age and grandeur.

Contemporary needlepoint rugs, like those made in Portugal, are a good alternative to antique rugs. It is, however, difficult to create a natural faded look with them and sometimes the designs and colours can dominate a room, forcing you to choose the colour scheme around the rug. I tend to use them more in hallways or bedrooms, or in a neutral area where they will be the main source of colour and design.

Another solution is to have a rug made up to your own design. Many good carpet manufacturers offer this service using either a cut pile or loop pile such as Brussels weave. It is a good solution for rooms of awkward shapes and sizes as the body of the rug and its border can be made to fit exactly.

Sisal, coir and sea-grass mats are hardwearing, practical and good looking, especially on wood, stone or tiled floors. They can be given a touch of colour with a binding to stop them fraying.

Whether laid on carpet, directly onto wood, tiled or stone floors, all rugs will need some sort of backing or underlay to stop them slipping and wearing out. As there are so many different types of backing, it is best to seek advice on this subject from an expert carpet fitter.

ABOVE *Hardwearing sisal flooring can be fully fitted in the same way as carpet. It is easy to clean and very practical, makes a good background for colourful rugs, and is not as hard and prickly underfoot as you might imagine.*

RIGHT *Needlepoint carpets like this one are now factory-made in Portugal, but were originally a Victorian home industry. The rugs were made from panels of needlepoint stitched together.*

FAR RIGHT *The typical rose-gold colours of French carpets of the early 19th century. The most beautiful of them came from the Aubusson and Savonnerie workshops. Like kilims, they are tapestry-woven, so they have no pile and are therefore fragile. Typical designs include stylized floral clusters and arabesques.*

THROWOVERS

Antique textiles can help add to the intimate atmosphere of a room. It can be something as simple as an old paisley shawl thrown over the back of a sofa, or an elderly rug elegantly draped over the side of a wing chair.

Unfortunately, antique textiles in all forms are becoming more and more sought-after and therefore more and more expensive even if you are fortunate enough to find the right piece.

SHAWLS

The most popular kind of antique throwover are Kashmir shawls which were first introduced into Europe in the late eighteenth century. They were made from the finest Himalayan goat hair and were traditionally decorated with the embroidered traditional motif known as 'boteh'. Early shawls were stole-shaped, later becoming square and rectangular. The designs were copied in Europe and machine made. One of the first replicas came

ABOVE AND RIGHT *Paisley shawls used as a bedspread (above) and covering a day-bed (right). The distinctive pattern derives from Indian textile designs. The characteristic shape is thought to derive variously from pinecones, palms, almond and cypress trees. Queen Victoria wore embroidered Kashmiri shawls with these designs, and thus started the fashion. These shawls were then woven in both Scotland and France.*

ABOVE *An antique rectangular paisley shawl with a cream ground used as a throwover on a modern canvas chair. Victorian shawls are fragile and should be treated with care.*

from Paisley in Scotland, and the name has stuck. Paisley is now synonymous with this type of woven design. These shawls and the paisley pattern continue to be popular; in fact there is a very strong revival of them at the present time.

BED AND TABLE THROWS

Antique throwovers can also be used as bedspreads. Even if they are not large enough to cover a whole bed, they can look effective as a square on top of a white lace or plain bedspread. Another use for throwovers is as a tablecloth, or an overcloth, to be removed when the table is required for eating. Old lace makes an attractive throwover, but is perhaps best suited to bedrooms, along with old quilts and delicate pieces of embroidery.

DECORATIVE CUSHIONS

Cushions soften hard edges, they add colour, comfort and style to any seating arrangement however formal or casual. A successful mix of cushions and upholstery requires a certain amount of restraint and an eye for shapes and patterns that complement one another.

Cushion covers can be made from contrasting or matching upholstery fabrics, from tapestry panels or embroideries or even from kilims or Aubusson rugs that have seen better days. Antique tapestry cushions have become increasingly popular over the past few years and consequently the prices have risen. As an alternative to the genuine article, some companies make small fabric panels, using antique tapestries as a pattern, at a fraction of the price of the real thing.

BELOW *A pair of needlepoint cushions and a pair of red damask ones arranged on a pretty little sofa with a rich red velvet throw. The combination is very effective.*

ABOVE *A mixture of* gros *and* petit point *cushions look particularly inviting and colourful. If your needlepoint is not up to scratch, woven reproductions are available.*

ABOVE *A variety of cushions made from modern printed cottons, bits of carpet and kilim, fragments of old tapestry and modern needlepoint. If you make your own cushions, save scraps of fringing and old braid to decorate antique fabrics.*

Plain fabrics can be used as contrasts to patterned fabrics but try to use the same weight of material; for instance, team a patterned chintz with a plain chintz, not a heavy linen. If the front of the cushion is very decorative, the back side will look much better plain, but again,

make sure the fabrics work together. If you have a tapestry on the front, use something equally robust like a velvet or a heavy linen on the back.

SHAPE AND SIZE

The dimensions of a patterned cushion will be dictated by the size of the motif. This is particularly important when dealing with a fabric or a rug designed to cover a large area. A fragment of a larger pattern will always look unresolved, whereas a small repeated motif will look at

home however small the cushion. A small scrap of tapestry or treasured embroidery can always be turned into a reasonably-sized cushion by adding a border of complementary fabric.

A variety of shapes, sizes and patterns is more pleasing to the eye and looks more welcoming and comfortable than a regiment of similar squares. A classic arrangement for a three-seater sofa is a symmetrical one of five cushions, consisting of two pairs and a single one in the centre. Armchairs, depending on size, look most inviting with just one or two cushions — too many and the sitter will feel crowded out.

Cushion pads, luckily, come in all shapes and sizes. The softest and most expensive are filled with down; the most reasonable with feather and down and lumpy ones to be avoided are filled with foam chips. Choose a pad an inch (2.5cm) larger than its intended cover for a full, plump-looking cushion, but if you like your cushions squashy and flat choose a pad the same size or even a little bit smaller. Altering the size of cushion pads can be a very messy business, so if you have a favourite cover that is of no discernible standard size, it is advisable to ask an upholsterer to make up the pad for you.

If you are making new cushion covers, I recommend where possible using zippered covers so they can be taken off and cleaned. Most antique cushions will have been stitched up by hand which involves unpicking and removing the cover for cleaning in order not to ruin the feather pad.

FAR LEFT The sumptuous look of rich embroidery on velvet. The gold braid and gold thread glow and glisten with Eastern promise.

LEFT Needlepoint cushions with distinctly Victorian designs of richly-blooming flowers on a dark ground.

TRIMMING

The more ornate the fabric, the simpler the trimming should be. An edging of cord or silk rope is an ideal way to frame an antique tapestry or embroidery. These days cords are available with a flange so they can be used like piping and do not need stitching on by hand. Floral chintz cushions look good with frills piped with a solid colour, and cushions made of sturdy fabrics like kilim rugs can take tassels and fringes with aplomb. Trimmings do not have to be confined to the edges. Plain fabrics can be made to look unique and interesting with panels or stripes of contrasting braids. Trimmings can be used with much effect to bring a disparate collection of cushions together, so they all have something in common and a reason for being grouped together.

OLD LACE

Pretty lace and linen pillows look lovely on a bed. Most antique lace was hand made and is quite exquisite in beauty and detail. It is also, not surprisingly, extremely delicate, very expensive and difficult to track down. A cheaper solution is to make up your own from remnants

ABOVE *Old linens and lace carefully stored in a well-ventilated cupboard. Old fabrics are best kept between layers of acid-free tissue paper and rolled rather than folded as the creasing involved in folding can weaken the thread.*

LEFT *A very neat bed with a regiment of starched white pillow cases and cushion covers. The sheet and pillows have been embroidered in a style known as cut work.*

ABOVE Pretty lace pillows make a focal point of the bed which could easily have disappeared into a sea of blue and white pattern on pattern.

you may pick up at antique fairs or to buy reproduction pieces which can look just the part, especially when intermingled with the real thing. Panels of antique lace can be made into decorative pillows by mounting the panel onto a piece of plain white or coloured backing fabric. Cream lace can look particularly rich if used with a pale coloured silk or satin backing chosen to tie in with the rest of the room.

There is nothing more attractive or inviting than a bed made up with an antique lace or linen bedspread with an abundance of old cushions in different shapes and sizes. The great advantage of using white is that it goes with everything and brings a cool and elegant feel into any bedroom setting.

CURTAINS

The fabric that drapes around the windows is usually the single most decorative item in any room. There are instances, however, when I think it is better to keep window treatments simple, in order to provide a balance with other features in the room.

It is important, too, not to forget what windows are for. They are there basically to let in light and provide a view to the outside. They need to be opened to let in fresh air and yet they need to be dressed to provide privacy at night and a certain degree of protection from the elements.

The first consideration is what type of treatment is best for a particular window: are plain curtains appropriate, does the situation call for full, luxurious curtains and a pelmet, or is it a window best dressed with a blind of some kind? Then there is the question of where exactly will the curtains or blinds hang in relation to the window and the space surrounding it: how much space is there above and below and either side of the frame, where will

ABOVE *My bedroom is in a loft conversion and the windows are set into a sloping wall. I wanted to use this particular fabric to surround the windows, but obviously curtains would have been an impossibility. These stiffened and shaped fabric frames are called lambrequins, and were, I think, the perfect solution to the problem.*

LEFT *These magnificently-proportioned windows are enhanced by these simple, yet opulent curtains with their imaginative padded headings and loops of rope. A conventional pelmet would have hidden the top of the windows and diminished their grandeur.*

ABOVE *A door leading into the garden requires no curtain but is certainly improved by being framed by this beautiful antique shawl draped over an old wooden pole.*

the tracks or poles be fixed, and will the window still open when all the curtain paraphernalia is in place?

IMPROVING PROPORTIONS

Where possible try not to lose the shape or character of any window. If the window has functioning shutters, then retain them and use them. If the window is arched, then emphasize it by following its shape with the curtain or pelmet.

Some windows do not look proportionally correct in relation to the room, and in these cases the window treatment can remedy the problem. For instance, if you have a short, squat window and a high ceiling, you can give the impression of a tall, graceful window by placing a pelmet

board high above the top of the frame and using long curtains and a deep pelmet, rather than emphasizing the bad proportions with short curtains placed on a track just above the frame. And if you have two windows of differing sizes on one wall, you can use curtain treatments to make them appear to be the same size.

TRACKS AND POLES

In this section, I do not intend to talk in great detail about curtain and blind making, as it is a lengthy and quite technical subject. There are, however, some basic decisions on the use of decorative accessories and curtain fabrics that can radically affect the look of your window treatments. The average curtain track is efficient, but plain and unattractive, so where possible I either conceal it or try to come up with a more decorative alternative. When using pelmets, this does not present a problem as the track is permanently hidden by the fabric

ABOVE *Full-length windows need the simplest of treatments.
These beautifully made curtains hang from an elegant
polished solid brass pole, running the length of the room.*

of the pelmet. If you are using conventional track and
wish to conceal it without going in for a pelmet, then the
simplest solution would be a covered fascia board. This
is a small frame fitted over the track, which can be covered in the same fabric as the curtains, and conceals all
but the hooks on the track.

WOODEN POLES

Curtain poles are one of the best alternatives to tracks.
Normally they have loose rings from which the curtains
hang, but they can be internally corded with the rings an
integral part of the pole, and these are a better solution
for heavy curtains or wide windows. Standard wooden
curtain poles are available in several wood finishes, or
painted white, and in diameters from about 1 inch to
$2\frac{1}{2}$ inches (2.5–5 cms). They usually come in a pack complete with wooden brackets and rings and can of course
be cut down to the exact size you require. I usually use
brass brackets with wooden poles, as I think they look
more stylish in most instances. However, if the pole is
painted, it is better to match the brackets to the pole.

Fatter wooden poles or poles with more exotic finishes are available from specialist companies supplying
plain, reeded, fluted or carved poles and a huge variety of
finials. Poles can be stained to match any wood finish,

painted to tie in with a particular scheme or even gilded
should the curtain treatment demand it.

It is not that easy to find old curtain poles, and if you
do, the chances are they will not be the correct size and
they may well be rotten. It is easy enough to distress
poles to look antique, and any book on paint finishes
will tell you how to do it.

BRASS AND WROUGHT IRON POLES

Brass poles look particularly good with large, heavy, dramatic curtains. Much the smartest brass finish is solid
brass, which can be polished and lacquered. New brass
poles can be a bit off-puttingly bright and glitzy, but they
will mellow beautifully with age. Gold anodized poles
are lighter in weight but their glitziness never dims and
the finish will eventually chip with wear. I would always
pick a wooden pole over a cheap brass one.

Wrought iron poles have a real country feel and I have
used them to good effect in old-fashioned kitchens, bathrooms and cellar rooms. If you cannot find a standard
one that you like, then a skilled craftsman will be able to
make one up to your design. The finish does not have to
be solid black; it can be antique black, verdigris or some
other coloured finish to blend in with your scheme.

BELOW *Dignified drapes. The pelmet is a length of shaped
material draped over a wooden pole. The overlong curtains,
on a track above the window, finish in pools on the floor.*

RIGHT *A stiffened and shaped pelmet is a good way of showing off an attractive curtain fabric with a large design, that might otherwise get lost in the curtain folds.*

BELOW *An elaborate swagged and fringed pelmet in a grand bay window. The whole room has a lovely muted feeling, the patterns and colours coming from the rugs and upholstery materials rather than the walls and curtains.*

WOODEN PELMETS

Carved wooden pelmets or curtain cornices date back to the eighteenth century, and in the grander houses they were gilded and very ornate. They were often designed by the architect to tie in with other features in the room. If the window was arched, then they were made to follow the curve. Sometimes they reflected a theme used in the decoration of the room: a gothic look, for instance, or Chinese pagoda style fretwork. It is difficult to find antique carved pelmets as, thankfully, many of the originals have remained in the rooms they were made for. Simple carved pelmets are easy enough to reproduce, but if you are looking for an ornate carved piece, then you will have to have one made. There are a number of specialist firms offering this service.

Plain wooden pelmets can be made up by a good carpenter to follow the shape of a cornice. The size of the pelmet should relate to the proportions of the window. In some cases all that is required is to bring the cornice out in front of the window to form a box under which the track can be fixed and the curtains hung. This is a

LEFT *A small, but elaborately carved, gilt wood corona holds a simple striped cotton bed hanging. The fabric is caught at the sides on carved gilt wood rods fixed to the wall.*

BELOW *In another bedroom in the same house, the coronas are more regal and brass arms are used to hold the fabric back at the sides. The rest of the furnishings are very simple.*

good solution for a wood panelled room, so the tracks or poles do not have to be fixed to the panelling.

BED HANGINGS

The term corona is used to describe the crown-like feature above a bed from which bed curtains will hang. They are usually confined to the bedroom but you may find them used as a feature over day beds in a sitting room or study. A half-tester serves a similar purpose but it is a different shape, a sort of rectangular box made to the width of the bed.

Bed hangings have been used for hundreds of years, but up until the late eighteenth century they were there for a purely practical reason: to keep out draughts. Throughout Europe in the late eighteenth century, furnishings became huge status symbols. No expense was spared and in the grandest homes coronas, half-testers and fourposters were lavishly carved and gilded to match the pelmets over the windows. In France it was fashionable to have a dome from which the bed drapes hung to heighten the sense of grandeur.

ABOVE *A beautifully simple American fourposter bed. The canopy is lined in white to match the curtains and the decoration on the canopy edge picks up colours from the quilt.*

LEFT *This charming little 18th century French-style bed alcove is draped with back-to-back brocades and classic floral chintzes hanging from a simple square corona.*

The fabrics used for these elaborate bed hangings were silks, damasks, brocades and taffetas usually trimmed with hand-knotted silk ropes and tassels. Apart from being horrendously expensive, the effect would be overwhelmingly out of place today. But there is no need to go that far. If you want a draped bed, use cotton fabrics, both plain and patterned. Generally speaking, the patterned fabric is for the outside curtain, and the insides and back are lined with a small co-ordinating pattern or are plain. Trim and edge the fabric with plain fabric or braids, fringes and fan edges. The most important consideration is the relationship between the size of the bed and the size of the room.

Copies of original carved wooden coronas and half-testers are fairly easy to find. Many companies who make curtain poles will be able to supply them. Another alternative would be a brass copy, which comes with rings on which to attach the curtains. The simplest solution of all is a piece of shaped chipboard, covered in fabric.

USING ANTIQUE TEXTILES

Antique fabrics add a certain atmosphere and a sense of the past which is difficult to recreate with new fabric. As a result, antique curtains and remnants of old textiles have become increasingly fashionable and it is becoming more difficult to find them, especially lengths that are in good enough condition to use.

Old textiles are very fragile. Light, dust, pollution, and the wrong type of cleaning will all have helped speed up their deterioration, so to prolong their life they must be handled with care. Use old curtains in an area where they will not be exposed to much sunlight. If the edges are already frayed, they can be turned back and the hems

LEFT *This characterful, colourful curtain is made from an old kilim rug, with a pocket sewn across the top to accommodate a slender wooden curtain pole supported by brass fittings.*

RIGHT *A beautiful old curtain embroidered with the Tree of Life design. It has been carefully attached to an inner curtain that takes all the strain of the curtain tape and hooks and also protects the antique fabric from the fading glare of the sun.*

BELOW *A stunning bedroom curtain of old crochet lace. On the table are two Victorian beaded pincushions.*

taken up (assuming they are large enough). Getting them cleaned by a specialist firm and changing the lining and interlining will help preserve them, but if the fabric looks too delicate to unstitch, it would be wiser to leave them as they are.

MODERN FABRICS

Fortunately there are some wonderfully lush fabrics still woven today which do imitate many of the old-fashioned damasks, taffetas, silks, brocades, velvets and chenilles.

The richness and depth of the colours are probably not the same and, for reasons of cost and practicality, the fabrics will undoubtedly have a fair percentage of man-made fibres.

There are a few remaining factories, both in England and in Europe, that still hand-weave fabrics, and there is no doubt that the quality of these speak for themselves. With good quality craftsmanship, and a good supply of antique poles, accessories and trimmings picked up from auctions and antique shops, it is possible to reproduce

LEFT *A wonderful old damask curtain that is proudly showing its years. Professional conservation of fabric sometimes entails the application of a very, very fine gauze overlay to prevent further disintegration. The beautiful tasselled rope tieback is an antique too.*

BELOW *This heavy white brocade curtain is looped over a tieback made from a piece of exquisite Victorian braid trimmed with hand-made silk flowers.*

antique curtain designs, and indeed it is happening all the time during the renovation of historic buildings. However it is an expensive business.

A way of achieving a grand, classic feel without breaking the bank is to spend your money on trimmings and accessories, using an inexpensive plain linen fabric for the actual curtains. I often think that it is the accessories that make a curtain treatment: beautiful fringes and rope tassel tiebacks can make plain, but generously cut, curtains look absolutely stunning.

TRIMS AND TIEBACKS

Curtains should be hung properly and dressed so they look good both open and closed. Tiebacks are useful here in helping to dress curtains when they are drawn.

ABOVE *The retaining arms that hold back these impressive red curtains have been stained or painted to match the dark wood. The curtain poles are almost invisible.*

Most curtain trimmings – ropes, fringes, braids and such like – will have matching tiebacks. They will probably be made of rope with either one or two tassels or without any tassels at all. Tassels vary greatly in style, complexity and cost, and obviously the more intricate the design, the more expensive they will be.

Brass arms or rods can also be used to hold the curtain loosely back. Rods, if made of wood, can be fabric covered, perhaps with a bow or rosette on the front.

Whatever the style of tieback, it should be placed at the correct height in relation to the height of the window, and while this is to a certain extent a matter of personal taste, somewhere below half-way down usually looks best. The position of the hooks that hold the tieback is another important factor. The outside hook should be in line with the outside edge of the curtain, and you may find it better to have two hooks on each side for larger curtains, especially when using bulky rope tiebacks. Tieback hooks are available in a variety of forms and sizes, and it is relatively easy to find old ones, although they do not really need to be that decorative, as they will rarely be noticed.

Once the tiebacks are in place, you can dress the curtain to scoop over the tieback and give more fullness. I like to make curtains long when using tiebacks, so that the outer side will still touch the floor when tied up.

FABRIC ON WALLS AND CEILINGS

Using fabric directly on walls is a traditional method of decoration and dates back many centuries. It has always been popular in grander houses: in particular in France and other parts of Europe. Today, using fabric in this way has become fashionable and, while it is more expensive than either paint or wallpaper, it does have some practical advantages. Fabric can cover imperfections in walls and ceilings and it will help insulate against sound and heat loss while giving a warm and inviting feel.

WHAT KIND OF FABRIC?

Use only flame-retarding fabrics that have been treated with a solution to help protect them from grime, dust, smoke and excess light. Most fabrics will fade in direct sunlight anyway. Not all fabrics are suitable for wall hanging, they may stretch too much or the design might not be suitable. Stripes are a case in point as they are very difficult to align. Damasks, silks and moirés all look

ABOVE *In this magnificent drawing room, the walls are covered with silk damask fabric and the cornices and pilasters that hide the raw edges are of wood with a faux marble finish. Note the white blinds at the windows that keep out the sun's damaging rays.*

LEFT *A warm, welcoming and exotic den with walls hung about with paisley shawls and a pleated, tented ceiling. The furniture and pictures are also suitably oriental.*

RIGHT *A wall of rich red damask. The edges of the fabric are concealed by ornate gilded fillets.*

wonderful but are very expensive and, as they will inevitably fade and rot in the sunlight, you will have to install blinds or shutters to protect them.

Rich, dark colours such as reds, greens and golds look particularly good with oil paintings hung on them and as a background to antique furniture. You do not have to use fabric on the whole height of the wall. In fact, it often looks best running from dado height to below the cornice. The wall below the dado can be painted to contrast or tie in with the fabric colour.

ATTACHING FABRIC TO THE WALL

Paper-backed fabrics can be stuck directly to the wall, as can some fabrics like felt. The edges can be finished off with a braid or some other type of trim.

The more traditional way of hanging fabric is by battening the walls and first applying an interlining followed by the fabric which has been sewn together in panels. The edges can again be finished with rope, braid or a gilt or wooden trim. This is not an easy DIY job, as it is hard to get the fabric well stretched and the design straight. I would always recommend using a professional.

An easier method is called 'Fabritrack', which entails lining the wall with plastic strips and tucking the fabric behind them. It results in a clean edge which requires no finishing braid or trim.

BELOW *The fabric on these walls has been draped onto the walls to echo the draped pelmet.*

ABOVE *Striped silk moiré on the walls has a definite sheen and glow about it that wallpaper can never match.*

Fabric can also be pleated onto walls or ruched or shirred onto rods placed at the top and bottom of the wall. Obviously these methods are more expensive as they require more fabric and, although they look very effective, they are harder to clean.

TENTED CEILINGS

Fabric can be used on ceilings in much the same way as on walls: for practical as well as aesthetic reasons. You can lower a high ceiling with a fabric tent or a suspended panel of fabric. You can soften a hard, cold-looking room or create an intimate atmosphere in just one area, and, on a practical note, you can also help insulate against sound and heat loss.

In my view, tented ceilings should be used sparingly, to accentuate a particular area. This could be an alcove or dining area that needs to be visually separated from its surroundings.

The fabric can be stretched flat and battened from one side to another. For a tent effect the fabric needs to be

ABOVE *A room that is uncompromisingly Scottish baronial gothic. The walls are tartan clad and the ceiling fabric has been gathered onto poles and taken to a central point.*

shirred onto poles around the walls and gathered to a central point on the ceiling. The height and style of the subsequent tent will vary according to the available height and the size of the area.

This is the method used for the ceilings of fourposter beds, and traditional decorative ideas for trims such as rosettes, frills and bows can be borrowed from the fourposter to finish the top and edges of your tented ceiling.

Lightweight fabrics such as muslin can look effective draped from the ceiling. Muslin is also reasonable in price, so you can afford to use a lot of it, and it will let light filter through if you have the problem of roof lights to contend with.

CARE OF WALL AND CEILING HUNG FABRICS
Fabric can be vacuumed to keep it free from dust, but be careful not to apply too much suction as it may stretch. Fabric can also be brushed with a clean, long-handled broom as long as it is not a fabric with loose strands.

CARE AND REPAIR OF ANTIQUE TEXTILES
Antique textiles will deteriorate if exposed to extremes. Dry conditions will cause brittleness, damp will result in mould and too much sunlight will fade and rot delicate

fabric. If pieces of fabric are to be displayed, then temperatures and conditions should be kept constant. Small, delicate items should be displayed behind glass to help protect them from the elements. Any paper or board used to mount or protect the textiles should be acid-free and attached in a way that will not damage the cloth once removed.

Store textiles flat to avoid creases. If the fabric has to be folded or rolled, then use acid-free tissue paper, fold loosely and pad well. If the fabric in question is a garment, then hang it on a wooden, not a metal, hanger and cover with a calico bag, not a plastic one, so the fabric can breathe.

Any precious garment or piece of antique textile that requires repair or cleaning should be taken to an expert for a consultation, as dry cleaning may suit one fabric but do dreadful damage to another. For example, it is always better to hand wash white cotton and linen items, however old they are, in a mild soap. They will come up much whiter than if dry cleaned.

With every cleaning, textiles will become more delicate. Firstly, remove all dust by vacuuming or gently brushing then, if necessary, have any spots or stains removed by professional cleaners. This advice applies equally to rugs.

BELOW *Another way to enjoy fabric in a room is to cover a screen with it. This fabric-panelled screen protects a cosy reading corner from draughts.*

BATHROOMS

THE MAIN REQUIREMENTS FOR BATHROOM EQUIPMENT HAVE
CHANGED VERY LITTLE OVER THE YEARS, BUT PEOPLE'S
EXPECTATIONS OF COMFORT HAVE RISEN SHARPLY. THE COMFORT
FACTOR LIES IN THE DETAILS – THE HOT TOWEL RAILS, THE WARM
SURFACE UNDERFOOT, WELL-LIT MIRRORS, ATTRACTIVE JARS OF
SOAPS OR SHAMPOOS AND A GENERAL FEELING
OF PAMPERING THE SENSES.

THE FITTINGS

Bathrooms, as we would recognize them today, came into existence in the nineteenth century. Before that, every bedroom had a bowl, a water jug and, when required, a tin bathtub was set in front of the fire and filled by hand. Plumbed-in bathrooms were considered a luxury and initially only found in the grander houses. Once pipework and hot water storage tanks were installed inside houses, then rooms were set aside for the business of bathing.

Today, many of the old designs for sanitary ware have been revived, and the trend for Victorian style bathrooms with free-standing fittings and some exposed pipework is becoming increasingly popular. The variety of bathroom fittings is enormous and your decisions will be governed firstly by your budget and the space available, and secondly by your individual taste. When considering your budget, bear in mind that for a bathroom it is always worth spending that little bit extra to buy good quality fittings that last and retain their looks. Genuine antique fittings, should you decide to go for authenticity, need careful installation and subtle updating, but can work well in a modern setting.

BATHS

Once they no longer had to be carried from room to room, baths were made of glazed stoneware, but the material was soon abandoned in favour of enamelled cast iron which retained the heat of the bath water. Early bathtubs were generally painted with elaborate designs and the top covered with a wooden casing to make it look more like a piece of furniture. The more practical cast roll rim and square corners were introduced later.

By about 1910, cast iron baths were enamelled with porcelain enamel: a very hard coating fired onto the

RIGHT *A pretty Victorian bathroom with a restored and renovated cast iron bath. Reproduction brass taps with porcelain inlays are a better bet that the real thing, as they are precision engineered and conform to all the required plumbing standards. The exposed pipes, an authentically Victorian feature, have here been brass plated to make them more attractive.*

LEFT *Even in an awkwardly-shaped tiny bathroom, the free-standing Victorian look can work. Well-made modern reproductions of cast-iron Victorian baths and porcelain sinks are available through good bathroom equipment specialists.*

metal and much more durable than the previous painted enamel coatings. The pressed steel bath was introduced in the 1950's. Then followed acrylic baths and coloured suites, a trend which is fortunately diminishing. For while acrylic baths are light and cheap, they are not durable and they do not feel good to bath in. Coloured suites are all very well, but white is so much more versatile and colour can still be brought into the room with decoration and accessories.

ANTIQUE BATHTUBS

Old baths will most likely be chipped and require re-enamelling. This can be done reasonably successfully, but make sure the job is carried out by a good company prepared to give you a long guarantee. The tap holes on an old bath will probably not accommodate new taps, so you may have to buy antique taps as well. Make sure that your plumber knows what he is doing and provides suitable connections from old fittings to new pipework.

LEFT *A custom-built vanity unit covered with mosaic tiles. The inset washbasins are modern but the effect is decidedly Victorian because of the Victorian-style tiles and wallpaper, the ferns and the Staffordshire pottery dogs.*

WASHSTANDS

Portable washstands have been in existence since the early eighteenth century. They developed from the purely practical into elegant and attractive pieces of furniture once they were given the attention of famous cabinetmakers such as Chippendale and Hepplewhite. Early versions were designed to sit permanently in a corner of a room and they housed a bowl, soap dish and mirrors so they could be used as a shaving stand. Later versions became more elaborate and were a combination of dressing table and washstand, housed in one cabinet, which when closed looked like a beautiful piece of furniture. And that is really how they should be appreciated today. They just are not sufficiently practical for today's warm and steamy bathrooms.

MARBLE TOPS AND SPLASHBACKS

More practical washstands with marble tops and splashbacks were introduced around 1830. Initially the bowls and jugs sat on top of the stands with a slop pail hung below. Once plumbed-in water was available, the design remained much the same, only the bowl was sunk into the marble top and a wooden casing was used to conceal the pipes.

CERAMIC BASINS

Porcelain basins and pedestal basins first appeared around 1900, once the techniques of slip casting had been perfected. The fashion in those days was for white basins with shiny chrome taps and exposed pipework. This is a look that is still valid today.

The first decision you have to make about washbasins is whether you want a free-standing pedestal or a wall-mounted model with a built-in vanity unit. If you want a Victorian look, find an old marble washstand to convert into a vanity unit. You just have to get the top cut out to house the basin and the taps and their attendant plumbing can be set into the wall behind.

WATER CLOSETS

The history of the water closet, or lavatory, goes back a long way. As far back as 1449 the Englishman Thomas Brightfield came up with a flushing cistern, and in 1596, the Elizabethan courtier and part-time poet, Sir John Harington, invented another example. But as there was no running water to flush through these cisterns, no use could be found for them. What people used were chamber pots pushed under the bed or, in grander homes, housed in elegant pot cupboards.

In the Georgian era, sanitary conditions gradually improved as drains and sewers were built in towns, and piped water was connected to grander homes. From 1700 onwards, a variety of flushing systems were developed along with designs for closets, and by 1840 most homes had one in some form or another.

Pedestal lavatories were quite elaborately decorated, both inside and outside. The seats were usually polished mahogany and the tanks were decorated to match the pan. But beware of buying an old lavatory unless it already has a seat. It is difficult enough to find new wooden seats to fit new lavatories, let alone old ones.

RIGHT *An elegant cage of brass-plated pipework makes both a shower and a curtain rail.*

FLOORS, WALLS AND WINDOWS

Bathrooms need to be practical but not too clinical. An all-white bathroom with white tiles or white marble on the walls and floor would be fine in an all-year-round hot climate but when days are cold and dreary you want the bathroom to be warm in both temperature and atmosphere.

This is where wall and floor finishes come in. They not only need to be suitable but also aesthetically pleasing. Carpet, for instance, is wonderful underfoot, but it is just not practical in a small bathroom with a shower, nor in a bathroom used by children. A tile or vinyl floor

LEFT *The boxed-in modern cast iron bath has a good wide shelf all around, very useful for bathing paraphernalia. Where bathrooms are not overlooked, it is a lovely idea to be able to bath while enjoying the view.*

BELOW *A genuine antique basin and taps installed in an old house with rough plastered walls. The walls and floor have been stencilled in suitably muted colours.*

ABOVE *In a whitewashed attic room of an old castle, a collection of commemorative royal mugs adds a bit of colour and wit.*

would be more serviceable with large bath mats providing colour and comfort.

For the walls, paint is perhaps the best solution. Tiles can be clinical, especially if used all over. It is perhaps best to use them only in areas where necessary, and to use a patterned tile or plain tiles with a border for added interest.

Wallpaper will certainly add colour and warmth, but again it is not a practical solution for a small bathroom with poor ventilation where the build-up of condensation will cause it to peel off.

WINDOWS

Curtains and blinds are another way of bringing colour into the room, and curtains can be decorative even if they are not strictly necessary. Obviously the window treatment you choose will depend on the shape, size and position of the window, and whether you are overlooked or not. If you do have a wonderful view, then it would be a shame to hide it forever behind obscure glass. But if all you have outside your window is a tangle of your neighbours' pipes, then there are some very pretty patterns available in obscure glass copied from old designs which, although more expensive than the average reeded or bobbled glass, are infinitely more pleasing to the eye.

BATHROOM ACCESSORIES

RIGHT *An elegant bath/shower combination tap unit in lacquered brass. Old taps or reproduction taps really set the scene – the effect of this Georgian-style bathroom would be completely spoiled with taps of a modern design.*

BELOW *Taps with personality. A blue and white Chinese theme is carried through all the accessories from the soap dish to the hand towels.*

Once you have decided on the basic fittings and layout, it is the choice of accessories that is really going to make your bathroom individual.

Taps are one of the first considerations and the choice of finish – brass, chrome or perhaps nickel-plated – will determine the finish of the other accessories in the room. It is of course possible to mix them up – chrome taps and brass door furniture, for example – but it is better to stick to just one.

Most taps are made from cast brass and then plated to produce a finish. Plated finishes are much easier to keep clean than brass but they should not be rubbed with abrasive creams or cloths. Old brass taps and non-lacquered brass will tarnish easily and need a lot of polishing to keep clean, but if this tarnished look is one you want to achieve, then these are the fittings to choose.

TOWEL RAILS

Heated towel rails are essential in a bathroom, and if there is no room for a radiator then this is the perfect way of heating the room and keeping your towels warm and dry. They can either be connected to the central heating system and combine a radiator with a rail, or connected to the hot water system, providing warmth all year round even if your central heating is turned off.

Alternatively you can have an electric towel rail fitted that you can switch on and off at will.

Heated rails are available in all finishes, including white, and can be wall or floor mounted. Once covered with towels you will hardly notice them so they will rarely be an eyesore taking up valuable space, which a radiator on its own can easily be.

Old-fashioned free-standing wooden towel rails are attractive accessories, but not terribly practical unless you can position them in front of a radiator or other source of heat to dry the towels.

CHAIRS AND TABLES

If you have the space, then I think it is always a good idea to include a chair in a bathroom. It is often an ideal spot for relaxing and chatting to someone and it is also a useful resting place for clothes or dressing gowns.

Occasional tables are both pretty and useful. They can

ABOVE *In this elegant 1930's-style bathroom, two chrome heated towel rails, designed to be fixed to the wall, have been fixed together to form a large, box-shaped towel rail behind the bath.*

RIGHT *A plain, Shaker-style wooden towel rail holds a towel at the ready in this elegant gentleman's bathroom.*

RIGHT *This small, neatly fitted bathroom has been given many added dimensions through the use of mirror glass panels fixed to all available wall space up to picture-rail height.*

be used to display attractive bottles, baskets of soap, sponges and loofahs or purely decorative touches such as a collection of shells.

CUPBOARDS, SHELVES AND RACKS

Shelves and wall cupboards need not be unattractive plastic boxes with mirrored fronts. Old wooden shelves, either polished or painted and picked out to match your scheme, can brighten up a bathroom considerably, and an antique cupboard will make a room look more cosy than a plain white one. For a more modern look, glass and perspex shelves and accessories are a good alternative, and they can be used with either brass, chrome or painted metal or wooden brackets.

Bath racks, I think, tend to be more decorative than useful. There are times when they just get in the way. The old, heavy ones can look good on a large, old bath, especially if it is a free standing bath and there is no handy shelf or ledge for the soap and the rubber ducks.

Another essential is a hook on the back of the door for hanging dressing gowns or towels. Nice, large antique hooks can be found in most markets or antique shops and are preferable to modern ones.

MIRRORS AND LIGHTS

Mirrors and good lighting are essential in a bathroom. Lighting must be shadow-free and sufficient for shaving and making up. Downlighters are perfect for the task, but if they are impossible to install, then use spotlights instead. In both cases, low voltage lights are the best, and a dimmer switch will mean you can alter the lighting to suit your mood.

Mirrors will always help reflect both natural and artificial light. Placed strategically they can make a small bathroom look larger. Where possible the basin should be placed against a wall on which a mirror can be hung. If the basin is set in front of a window, then you can either glaze the lower half of the window with mirror glass or fix an extendible swivel shaving mirror to the wall. Some shaving mirrors have integral lights.

KITCHENS

THERE IS A DEFINITE MOVE AWAY FROM THE IDEAL OF THE
GLEAMING FITTED KITCHEN TOWARDS A MORE RELAXED COUNTRY
STYLE WITH FREE-STANDING PIECES OF FURNITURE, AND A
PREDOMINANCE OF NATURAL MATERIALS OVER CHROME AND
COLOURED PLASTIC. THIS IS, OF COURSE, HOW KITCHENS USED TO BE,
AND THE STYLE DOES NOT SUIT EVERYBODY, NOR EVERY HOUSE, BUT
CLEVER ACCESSORIZING CAN MAKE EVEN THE NEATEST FITTED
KITCHEN A MORE FRIENDLY PLACE TO BE.

STYLE AND FUNCTION

Most people spend more time in their kitchens than in any other room of the house. The kitchen is a room in which many different activities are carried out, from homework to flower arranging, and it therefore deserves to be not just practical and functional but aesthetic and welcoming. It is because the kitchen of today has become the centre of the home rather than a utilitarian work place that our attitude towards its decoration has changed.

Kitchen planning is a very specialized discipline, especially if you are trying to plan for a number of functions to be crammed into one small space, but it is not one I intend to cover in this book. In this section I am going to concentrate on how to achieve different looks with the imaginative use of decorative accessories.

KITCHEN UNITS

The choice and style of kitchen units ranges from rustic wood to the clinical gleam of stainless steel, and in the

LEFT *Open shelving, an old but efficient gas stove and a sink unit are lined up here in a characterful Mexican kitchen.*

ABOVE *Country style does not mean sacrificing modern convenience for the sake of rustic charm. In this simple kitchen, old delft tiles surround a built-in oven.*

BELOW *French, Swiss and Austrian country-style kitchen shelves often have pretty shelf strips of scalloped paper or fabric. These shelves are edged with lace.*

end it is often a question of what is affordable rather than what you would really like. But you do not need to change the cupboards in order to change the style of a kitchen. For a new look, change the worktops and handles, or replace the door fronts or just re-paint them.

LAYOUT

The size of the room and the position of doors and windows will largely determine the layout. In my view, you do not require a large area for cooking. The three key areas: the preparation area, food storage and sinks should be laid out in a close triangle. You do not want to walk half a mile every time you make a cup of tea.

The style and layout of old-fashioned kitchens is becoming increasingly popular today. The trend is away from the total built-in look to free-standing furniture with a table in the middle of the room, a dresser housing everyday china, and pots and pans hanging from racks and hooks.

ABOVE *A modern, fitted country-style kitchen accessorized with silver and glass and some lovely old bits and pieces like the wooden egg stand and the hanging salt box. There are many antique dealers who specialize in old kitchen utensils and fittings because they are so attractive.*

RIGHT *An old kitchen dresser with ventilation holes in the doors so the food stored inside would benefit from circulating air. Originally these holes would have been covered with a fine mesh to keep out mice and other pests. The ceramic jars along the top are old chemist's jars and the balance is of the type used in shops at the turn of the century.*

ABOVE *A luxury in these times: a butler's pantry – not a place where food is prepared but where the wine is stored prior to serving at table and cellar books are written up.*

Every kitchen, however small, should try and incorporate an eating area, whether a simple breakfast bar or a separate table. The eating area can double as a food preparation area, but it should not get in the way of the work triangle or you will be tripping over it all the time. Another ideal space is a storage larder, if you have the room, where you can hide all the extra utensils and the useful but less than attractive bits and pieces that clutter up every kitchen.

And last, but not least, it is a nice idea to have a seating area in the kitchen with perhaps a television or an area where children can play safely while the work goes on.

COUNTRY KITCHENS

The kitchen of dreams and storybooks in these nostalgic days tends to centre around an Aga or old-fashioned stove. In town houses there is rarely the space to realize such dreams unless you can fit a stove into an existing open fireplace. In country kitchens they will add a cosy atmosphere and make an unbeatable focal point. If you are fortunate enough to have an old stove, then keep it. Even if it cannot be used for cooking, it can be used for storage or display.

An old stove or Aga set into a deep recess with, perhaps, an old exposed beam above, would make a wonderful decorative feature, especially if the recess is finished with old tiles and the beam or shelf is used to display antique kitchen objects.

Old beams will create atmosphere and also provide an ideal anchor on which to hang hooks for pots and pans and the *batterie de cuisine*. You can always install beams if you have not got any, and stain and distress them to look old or paint them to tie in with your kitchen units.

ABOVE *A lovely old country kitchen with free-standing wooden pieces and an old deep and square ceramic butler's sink. The painting is a charming naive 18th century family group. If you have an oil painting in your kitchen, make sure it is hung as far as possible from the cooker and is protected with an anti-bloom varnish.*

LEFT *With the addition of a tablecloth, this zinc-topped work table can be used for breakfasts and kitchen suppers. Above the pine sideboard, old mahogany hanging cupboards are used for storing glasses.*

RIGHT *Open shelves are much more practical than cupboards for storing pots and pans, because it is easier to get at them and easier to see what you are reaching for.*

TABLES AND CHAIRS

Kitchen tables and chairs need not bear any resemblance to your units, in fact it is better if they don't, as a surfeit of the same thing can look too systemized. Depending on the space available you can choose a kitchen table of the long refectory type, or a round, an oval, or a square, or even have one custom-built to fit the space. Whether you choose natural wood, painted wood or a glass-topped model, you can always change the look

RIGHT *At the eating end of a cottage kitchen, a mahogany table is set in front of the old kitchen range. Its built-in bread ovens and pot stand are a small reminder of just how hot and grim the chore of cooking once was.*

BELOW *An American refectory style table surrounded by American Windsor chairs.*

ABOVE *The eating alcove off the kitchen shown at the top of page 158. It has elegantly left out all references to the kitchen with its pretty French chairs and oval portraits.*

instantly with a tablecloth and mats. When not in use the table can double either as extra work space, or as a display area for books, plants, flowers or decorative china.

CHAIRS, STOOLS AND BENCHES
Chairs are more comfortable than stools or narrow benches, but if space is a problem, there is no reason why you could not use a combination. A long bench could be used on one side of a table, for instance, with chairs at the ends and along the other side.

Hard chairs can be made more comfortable and decorative with squab cushions tied on with bows and preferably with loose covers that can be taken off for washing. It is not necessary to keep all the chairs around the table all the time. Extra ones can be placed against a wall, or used in a hall and brought in when needed.

The style and finish of the chairs does not have to match the table. For example you could have a set of lovely antique yew Windsor chairs and use them with a modern pine or oak table.

STORE AND DISPLAY

For practical purposes, we tend today towards wall units with cupboard doors for reasons of hygiene and safety as well as to hide the mass of unattractive modern packaging. Decorative storage containers are a far more attractive alternative, and are perfect for storing dry goods such as tea, coffee, sugars, flour and cereals in optimum condition. Old storage containers are not practical in this context, because they will not be airtight, but there are many decorative modern containers available.

Although shelves do tend to accumulate dust and kitchen grime, it is worth having a few intermingled with your wall cabinets to display china or glass, maybe a collection of jugs or some other decorative collection. Shelves can help break up the monotony of a solid wall of cabinets, as can glass-fronted cabinets.

KITCHEN DRESSERS
Dressers are perhaps the ideal piece of kitchen furniture. Not only are they attractive, making a good focal point,

ABOVE *To be practical, storage jars have to be completely airtight for storing dry goods such as flour or sugar. Old storage jars will rarely fit the bill, but they look wonderful and can be used for hiding away all kinds of odds and ends that always accumulate in the kitchen. The jars on this wooden dresser are old salt-glaze storage jars.*

LEFT *A good looking selection of practical storage containers: preserving jars and stone glazed pots with tight-fitting cork lids. They are displayed in shelving that has been custom built from old wood. Built into the wooden wall on the left is a state-of-the art oven and a microwave.*

ABOVE *A generously-sized old pine kitchen dresser with a pull-out bread board offers plenty of storage space.*

LEFT *A far cry from laminated cupboard units, this lovely dresser is piled with early advertising memorabilia.*

but they provide a lot of storage, especially if they incorporate drawers and cupboards.

Antique dressers, either painted or in natural wood, will provide a pleasant contrast to built-in units. Alternatively, you can have one custom-built to fit a particular space and in the same finish as the rest of the kitchen. Dresser shelves are the ideal place for a small television or a stereo, for displaying a collection, or for keeping children's books and toys in an accessible spot.

DISPLAYING THE BATTERIE DE CUISINE

It is better to display items of the same finish together rather than split them up. For example, a set of copper

LEFT A decorative display of ancient and modern batterie de cuisine on an old-fashioned brass butcher's rail brings a touch of life to a pristine marble kitchen.

BELOW Gleaming and precise, these shelves get their character from the traditional shapes of the copper pans and the 1930's insulated teapot.

LEFT *An old pine plate rack is useful for drying plates and well as storing them. The perforated porcelain ovals leaning against the wall were originally used to put under meat on a meat plate, so the juices drain through.*

BELOW *Kitchen implements and moulds arranged with the care and attention to detail worthy of an artist.*

pots and pans will look more effective hung all together rather than dotted around the kitchen. Take into consideration the texture and colour of the background against which your collection will be displayed. Wooden items will get lost on a wooden dresser, whereas a collection of blue and white china will stand out and get noticed.

Storage units can be free-standing, like cast iron pot stands which can usefully fill an awkward corner, or plate racks which can sit on a work surface or be mounted with easy reach on the wall. With a bit of imagination, hooks can be fixed all over the kitchen to hang good-looking items like baskets, colanders, mugs and jugs.

BASKETS

In my kitchen I have used curtain poles attached to the base of a long shelf to hang baskets. By simply removing the ball ends, the baskets can be slipped on and off when required.

Baskets are useful for storage all over the house, but they come into their own in the kitchen where they can be used to hold anything from fruit, bread, vegetables and nuts to cutlery and corkscrews. They are fun to collect and because they are relatively cheap, it does not matter if they wear out with constant use.

KITCHEN COLLECTIONS

Choosing a collection for display in the kitchen is a matter of personal taste. The items need have nothing to do

LEFT *An old wood panelled kitchen. This deep china and silver cupboard is treated as a display cabinet for a collection of blue and white porcelain. The brass candelabra is a lovely piece that has been mercifully spared electrification.*

RIGHT *A dresser top used as a hanging cupboard shows off a china collection. It is appropriately festooned with garlic and dried flowers and topped with potted cheese jars.*

with kitchens or with cooking – graphic packaging, or doll's house furniture, for example. Some typical kitchen collections include cream jugs or teapots, a particular type of china, like blue and white or creamware, which looks good on dresser shelves or in a glass-fronted cabinet. Copper pots and pans, copper, china and glass moulds, old wooden cooking utensils, bread boards, cutlery trays all look good massed together – the list is endless. Equally you do not have to concentrate on one particular item, just collect individual pieces that appeal to you and catch your eye.

As with all rooms, it is you who have to live in your kitchen, and you who will know what best suits your taste and lifestyle and the way you like to cook and serve up food. Interior designers like myself can help by suggesting ideas and layouts you may not have thought of, and offer practical advice based on experience, but I am a great believer in letting each individual's taste be reflected in their own homes. A room, especially a kitchen, that is too 'designed' can end up with no heart or soul.

✳✳✳✳✳✳✳✳✳✳✳✳✳✳✳✳✳✳✳✳✳✳✳✳✳✳✳✳✳✳✳✳✳✳✳✳✳✳✳

INDOORS
AND
OUTDOORS

CONSERVATORIES, PATIOS AND TERRACES ARE PLACES WHERE
INDOORS AND OUTDOORS MEET, WHERE BOUNDARIES BETWEEN
HOUSE AND GARDEN ARE PLEASANTLY BLURRED. GARDENS
THEMSELVES BENEFIT FROM THE DECORATIVE TOUCHES OF STATUES,
URNS AND PLANTERS. INSIDE THE HOME, FLOWERS AND PLANTS IN
APPROPRIATE POTS CAN LOOK AS STUNNING AS A GREAT PAINTING.

✳✳✳✳✳✳✳✳✳✳✳✳✳✳✳✳✳✳✳✳✳✳✳✳✳✳✳✳✳✳✳✳✳✳✳✳✳✳✳

CONSERVATORIES

Agarden room or conservatory provides a natural link between house and garden, and at the same time gives you a room with a unique character in which you can use furniture and objects perhaps not suited to any other room in the house. The classic conservatory should reflect the look of an outdoor greenhouse, with plenty of nature's colours and textures.

I think it is a mistake to over-decorate conservatories with upholstered furniture and fussy window treatment. Leave the chintz curtains and elaborate details for other rooms. Conservatories should be filled with the plants for which they were originally planned. Furniture will look much more at home in these surroundings if made from wood, cane, wicker or perhaps wrought iron.

GLASS HOUSES

Window treatments are not necessary for aesthetic reasons, but may sometimes be needed for privacy, to cut

BELOW A lean-to conservatory has plenty of room for delicate plants to grow and thrive. The lightweight Lloyd Loom furniture can be taken into the garden on sunny days.

ABOVE An elegant garden room appropriately furnished with metal folding chairs, painted metal plant pot stands and some suitably botanical prints.

ABOVE *A motley selection of garden chairs in an informal rural conservatory-cum-greenhouse where garden work takes place alongside the friendly chaos of family meals.*

LEFT *A glazed-in back porch trailing with healthy greenery makes for a pleasing transition between indoors and outdoors.*

down on glare, or to block out a miserable grey day. Blinds are a functional and attractive solution, providing welcome shade from strong sunlight and a degree of control over the heat of the sun in summer and the loss of heat in winter.

Blinds made from a type of rattan, sometimes referred to as pinoleum, have the right indoors/outdoors feel. Wooden Venetian blinds look good too, and vertical blinds work well. Simple white roller blinds effectively provide privacy while letting natural light filter through. Nets and lace curtains can be used, although they will pick up a lot of grime, and untreated fabrics do have a tendency to rot in sunlight.

LIGHTING

There is often next to no wall space in a conservatory, so finding places to put furniture and lights can be a problem. And lighting is never just a practical consideration. It can be used to create atmosphere, to emphasize attractive features and pinpoint beautiful accessories.

LEFT *A lean-to conservatory built over an existing stone-flagged patio. Vines thrive very well in glass houses and this one not only provides a lovely display but protection from the heat of the sun in the summer months.*

RIGHT *An asymmetrical niche painted in faux marble with a utilitarian butler's sink for filling up the watering cans.*

BELOW *Candles, nightlights and lanterns make a magical setting for a dinner party.*

Different textures can be highlighted with floodlighting and colours warmed or cooled with coloured bulbs. At night, clever lighting can create wonderful shadows adding interest to a room full of reflective glass surfaces.

It is important, first of all, to decide on the room function and which features, if any, need to be lit. Conventional table lamps may suffice if your conservatory is used as a sitting room, but they are not always practical and the flex can get in the way.

For a dining room setting, wall or overhead lights fixed to the glazing bars and used on dimmers will be more appropriate, with candlelight to provide the atmosphere. For a reading or working light, standard lamps are a good alternative to table lamps, and can be easily moved around, providing you have enough sockets.

The choice and style of light fittings will depend on the style of the extension and the style of furniture. For instance if it is Victorian in style, then converted oil or gas lamps could be used. Uplighters, placed around the room, can be effective, especially if they are used to throw light up behind a plant or a statue. But remember that if the glass roof of your conservatory has no blinds, then the light will be reflected in the glass and can be quite dazzling.

A track with spotlights, preferably low voltage ones, can be attached to part of the roof and the spots angled to light groups of plants, furniture, or paintings. Depending on the type of bulb you select, you can either throw a flood of light to wash a wall or a direct spot to highlight something special.

Traditional outdoor-style wall lights and lanterns look good and, used with dimmers, can provide good atmospheric background lighting. Wrought iron fittings, painted in a colour to tie in with the surroundings, work well in conservatories, as do the Italian painted metal fittings often decorated with flowers, leaves and grape vines. You may also find you need an electric fan in the conservatory as with all that glass it can get very hot in summer.

Whilst dealing with the conservatory lighting, it is also important to consider what is going on in the immediate area outside. If you light up various plants, trees or focal points in your garden, you will add greater depth to the view from the conservatory at night.

FURNITURE

Cane, wicker and bamboo furniture is ideally suited to the conservatory, and today there are many different styles to be found, from the fat and comfortable to the elegant and upright. Antique cane or wicker furniture is difficult to find, and what there is, is generally in need of restoration. Many of the new styles are, in fact, copies of original designs, like Lloyd Loom chairs, and come in natural, stained or painted finishes. The most common colours are green and white, but others can work as long as they are not too strong. Green and white give a more traditional look; pastel colours reflect a more modern or *Art Deco* feel.

Personally, I prefer the natural colours of cane and wicker for conservatories, especially on larger pieces. Colour can be brought in with cushions and upholstery fabric. Painted pieces such as chairs, tables and shelves make pretty occasional pieces of furniture for bedrooms and bathrooms.

It is fairly easy to pick up cane, wicker and bamboo accessories such as magazine racks, tables, stools, shelves, hat stands and whatnots in junk shops. Try thinking of alternative, imaginative things to do with them. Laden with plants and hanging baskets, they can look just perfect in garden rooms.

WROUGHT IRON FURNITURE

Cast iron or wrought iron furniture will tend to give a Victorian or Edwardian feel to the room. It is very versatile in that it can be used both indoors and out. If used in a conservatory or garden room, I think iron looks better painted either white or green. Black, another common finish, can be a little harsh, especially if you are trying to achieve a light and airy look.

Iron chairs and benches will certainly need to be made more comfortable and inviting with feather-filled cushions. Foam cushions can be made to follow the line and form of the piece to define its shape, but they are not so comfortable.

Some wrought iron frames have seats of wooden slats, and the combination of the two materials can be attractive. The advantage of using wrought iron is that if your conservatory leads onto a patio or terrace, the furniture can be taken out on a sunny day, but beware: cast and wrought iron pieces are heavy to move!

LEFT *The covered veranda of a beautiful house in Queensland, Australia, where the major concern is to keep the sun out and the cool in. The painted wicker table and chairs are as bright and colourful as the flowers and the tablecloth.*

RIGHT *Somewhere to sit out on a sunny day: a little balcony swamped in wisteria.*

POTS AND PLANTERS

Plants are, of course, essential to the conservatory look, and it is very tempting to buy masses of them. Just remember that they do take quite a bit of looking after. Plants not only need suitable containers, they need to be located where you can get at them for watering without having to move a host of others or climb up ladders.

Plants can be displayed in just about any container as long as it is serviceable and leak proof —although minor leaks can be dealt with by lining the container with a plastic bag, or using a terracotta saucer without holes. The size of planter or container should be in proportion with the plant. A huge round container with a small skinny plant shooting out of the top will not do justice to either. The choice of planter can reflect other materials used in the room, blending in seamlessly, or it can be a complete contrast, designed as a feature.

BELOW Watering cans make delightful objects to have around, but they may not be terribly practical. Many will have been subtly damaged by rust along the seams, just enough for them to spring a slow leak.

ABOVE A portable herb garden in a classic Sussex trug – a split wood basket made for collecting flowers and vegetables from the garden. Little pots of herbs have been put into it and moss tucked all around to hide the edges of the pots.

PLACING THE PLANTERS

If you have an alcove in the conservatory, it will cry out for a decorative piece to be placed in it. This could be a statue or, in keeping with the garden theme, it could be an old stone urn with an exotic plant lit from below to provide more emphasis. For symmetry, use urns or planters in pairs. This can be an effective way of emphasizing a feature or a particular area. For example a doorway or a step can be indicated by placing plants either side. A seating area could be partitioned off to make a calm, private place by using a row of plants in pots or tubs acting as a screen.

CHOICE OF FINISH

Traditional garden planters are made from stone or terracotta. They can be simple in shape and form, or elaborately carved or sculpted. Shapes also very enormously, but the traditional garden flower pot shape, with its endless variations, is still popular. Long oblong planters are easily available, especially in terracotta, and they are ideal for windowboxes or along a run of wall space.

If you are using a lot of planters together, it is better to mix shapes and sizes rather than colours and finishes, or the pots will start to detract from the plants. To create a variety of height, place some planters on tables, hang others from hooks and beams, and choose plants of different heights and leaf shapes.

Wooden planters can be painted, left natural, or

ABOVE *A grand garden room as a summer sitting room suitably furnished with natural materials and dominated by flowers and plants.*

stained. If you are going to paint them, stick to simple colours that relate to other pieces in the room. Ceramic, metal and *tôle* planters tend to be more decorative than the stone or terracotta kinds but the simpler ones can look good. Fine porcelain, delicately-painted cachepots and ornate Chinese-style vases are best used in other rooms, leaving the more rustic pieces for the conservatory. Heavier pots not only look more suitable, they are much less likely to get knocked over and smashed on hard conservatory floors, and it is unlikely that a precious piece will be noticed or even appreciated among so many others.

Baskets of all types can make interesting and inexpensive plant holders, providing they are used with a liner. Baskets are also recommended for hanging as they are so lightweight.

GARDEN ACCESSORIES

Furniture and decorative items for the garden need to be more durable than those used for a conservatory, especially if they are to be left outside all year round. Again natural products made from stone, wood, iron or terracotta are much more attractive than man-made plastics and resins, and they will eventually weather and blend in harmoniously with the garden. If you do not want to move furniture in and out, your options are really limited to wrought or cast iron, hardwood or stone. Decorative cushions and tablecloths can be used to add comfort and a more welcoming feel.

PLANNING SPACES

Accessories are an important part of garden planning. They can be used to fill in gaps and to draw the eye towards a focal point. The layout and planning of a garden should be treated in much the same way as you would go about planning space in a house. As in a house,

ABOVE *A very stylish modern grouping of white canvas deck chairs with black glazed cotton cushions. The beautiful stone-flagged terrace is a maze of clipped box and obelisks.*

LEFT *Lunch al fresco under a shady tree surrounded by pots of flowering bulbs. It is important in a garden to have defined areas. This makes even the smallest garden more interesting.*

ABOVE *A perfect spot from which to contemplate the cultivation of one's garden. This is a beautiful, classic bench of 18th century design.*

LEFT *A garden pavilion in the gothic style welcomes the garden to come creeping in. The mural can be enjoyed from the garden with a practically unrestricted view.*

different areas will suit different purposes and each area should have a character that can be emphasized with a combination of decorative features, plants, trees and structures. Changes in texture will also help to define areas, such as gravel against grass, or paved areas next to brick, but sometimes they can look unfinished unless a detail is added.

URNS AND TUBS ETCETERA

Avenues of trees or walks though a garden may automatically draw your eye down a path, but you need something for the eye to focus upon and you may need a pair of urns or some other ornament, such as a matching pair of statues, to indicate the start and the finish.

In areas where flowerbeds may not be appropriate,

tubs and urns, filled with a variety of plants, can add colour and life. There is nothing more attractive than an Italian or French style courtyard with a mass of urns, tubs and hanging baskets overflowing with a sea of colour. The advantage of tubs is that you can change the flowers according to the seasons to ensure a mass of colour all year round.

In small, terraced town gardens the use of tubs is essential, as it is often the only way to introduce colour and greenery. Windowboxes are also a good way of livening up a dreary city window, and perhaps giving the city dweller an occasional scent of the countryside.

Sundials can look very attractive, particularly if they can be placed where four walkways meet. Old water pumps and boot scrapers look good, perhaps placed outside a back door. Old garden implements, impractical for use today, look good hung on walls, and old watering cans, conveniently placed outside the kitchen door, make good containers for plants or herbs. Stone water troughs are also good for herbs and bedding plants as they are long and shallow, and could be a perfect fit under a long, low window.

LEFT *Half-barrels are heavy when filled with soil, so make sure you know where you want them before you start planting.*

BELOW *A turn-of-the-century tiled windowbox, planted with the care of a flower arrangement.*

ABOVE *An unusual terracotta planter decorated to look like a basket.*

RIGHT *A formal pair of stone obelisks mark the entrance to the stone-flagged patio from the steps.*

BELOW *This lovely stone urn in the gardens of Sissinghurst, Kent has a dark backdrop of clipped box.*

ABOVE *An old stone sundial, classically positioned at the meeting of four walkways.*

RIGHT *An 18th century stone statue of Pomona, a Roman nymph who was supposed to preside over gardens and to be the goddess of all kinds of fruit trees, particularly apples. She stands in front of an ivy-clad Chilstone urn, flanked by pyramids of box.*

FOUNTAINS AND PONDS

The sound of running water always adds a certain peaceful atmosphere to a garden. You do not need a great deal of room for a fountain, and you do not have to locate it dangerously where children and pets may fall in. Fountains can be made in raised basins or situated against a garden wall. They can be custom-built to suit a certain location or selected from a vast range of standard products.

Sunken pools can be free form, lined with a plastic liner and the edge covered with a stone coping or rocks. If the pool is to have running water or a fountain included, then you need a recycling pump and an electricity supply. You may also like to consider some form of underwater lighting.

ABOVE *The gardens of the Villa d'Este in Tivoli, Italy were laid out in the late 16th century. This lovely fountain has become completely encrusted with moss. The mossy effect is easier to achieve if your fountain is sited in a shady place, as full sun kills moss and algae.*

LEFT *A charming natural stream with lush, overgrown banks, gets neatened up and formalized as it progresses through this magnificent garden.*

ABOVE *Old stone ages naturally because the natural imperfections and indentations in the surface provide good sticking points for mosses and lichens to get a grip. Re-constituted stone, from which a lot of modern garden statuary is made, has a smoother surface, so if you wish to emulate those aged patches of lichen, intervention is required. Applications of live yoghurt will encourage moss to grow.*

RIGHT *Visiting the grand gardens of stately homes can often inspire ideas for the domestic garden. This pond could be translated into a small garden, surrounded by old bricks and cobbles.*

Reproduction fountains are usually made of re-constituted stone or of lead, and occasionally marble. The first thing you will want to do to re-constituted stone is to age it. Try painting the surface with yoghurt.

On the subject of algae, you will inevitably get it in the water. For fountains you can use chlorine but for ponds you might consider the natural oxygenating properties of aquatic plants, and maybe a goldfish or two.

ABOVE *Water plants, like soil plants, have varying requirements. Some thrive with their roots completely submerged, others just like them to be a little damp. The lilies at the centre of the group have been planted on a platform.*

INDEX